D0363961

British Kings & Queens

British Kings & Queens

From the Anglo-Saxons to the House of Windsor

Sandra Forty

COMPENDIUM

Published in 2009 by
Compendium Publishing,
43 Frith Street, London W1D 4SA,
United Kingdom.

COMPENDIUM

Copyright © 2009 by
Compendium Publishing Ltd,
43 Frith Street, London W1D 4SA

ISBN: 978-1-9063-4736-9

Designer: Mark Tennent

All Internet site information provided
was correct when provided by the
Author. The Publisher can accept no
responsibility for this information
becoming incorrect.

Printed and bound in China

Contents

Page 1: Stephen is crowned king of England.
History Department, UCL via Jo St. Mart

Pages 2–3: George I at the Battle of Dettingen, June 27, 1743
George II became the last British king to lead his troops into battle.
Bridgeman Art Library/Getty Images 57297566

Left: Mary Queen of Scots loses at Langside, 1568. *The Art Archive/Galleria d'Arte Moderna Milan/Gianni Dagli Orti AA367804*

Ethelwlstus filius eadberti
regnaud pp annis hic in
certre prould fuit exprosint
hedib; filius distincerebz; post
medui necesitate expulsus i
regulariua regnid suscept
hc espulit semmr de ecchia
gens: Ss: Bacet ui caris spoud
gens spandalos ci Fresu uiu
ouduem domnoup aug tetia

Ethelbaldus filius dethelwls
reg: regni sw anni:

Edredus rer fil: edelwls
rer regni ppr: anni:

Elfredus filius edelwls
iumor; q regni uictons olt
aleone pe asto boue sussie
pax regnaudo ppp: annis
unim one sepuli: t ecca bi
par de hisul:

Edwardus rer fil: ei regna
uit: ppp: anni: sepult: i abd
q t pax fuut si mouasterio:

Elstani rer regnaute
sptii: annis: obut cluencstri
est:

Edmund rer ff: ei regnaui
vii: annis: pgressu tempis ad
latrone Sicta coufessus occu
buit: sepultus apd glestoui:

Edredus rer ff: ei
sepult: apud winti

Edwinus fil: edmuldi regni
ui anni: sepult: apd winton
i nouo mouasterio

Edgarus rer ff: ei regni
annis sepultus glestoue

Edwardus rer fil: ei regnau
im: anni: apd glous ei stelle
uouice sue post pnagio t bi
sia psalua pstarilus fuerat
trausfossus obiit: sepultus e
cu houore apd sefresbir

Ethelredus filius edgari re
regnaud ppm: anni: sepult:
e t ecca sci paili loudoue

Emildus rer ferreu laus
regnaud: s: anni: sepulte apd
glestonia

Cnutus rer danus regnan
pp: anni: sepule apud wiut
onua:

Haraldus rer filius ei regnau
iii: anni: sepultus est: apud
sem clement loudoue

Hardecnutus rer
regnaute: ii: anni: se
wutouia

Edwardus scs filius ebelred
reg: regni: ppui: anni: sepult
apud westm

Haraldus fil: godewi rer no
regnans octisus aute est i bello
t e sepult apd walcham

Willus panus e d: bastard regni
ppp: anni: obiit in noruandi sepil
capud eadem

Willus rer Ruffus filius eui
regulatur: pep: annis: q senela
occisus sepulte e apud wite
mi: anuo: pp regni sui estate
uius ei saugius aquo distan
cue os fuuchastuse nbar
rodire obulite post her aigue
cessi mei uocte est ardere

Heuricus frater ei rer regnau
ppps: anno: nouens in Nor
mauui: sepulte apud rodug:

Stpps rer filius alie secoris
reg heuri rer: anni: sepultus
e in diadhua de succesuu

Heuricus filius imptricis
maue ppp: anni: sed thomt
archep canuaru passiis est
martirium: dano: p: lpps
ifs: obut rer: sepult apud fou
tem euraldi:

Ricuuus filius su
re: ah patri sepult
ace thoui archisi
pi epil thr:

Godirdus rer filus eius reg...
anis: sepultus e: apd...

Iohanues frater eius rer...

Heuricus rer filius regis Joh...
regnaud: lyu: anni: obiit...

Edwardus filius regis heuria

Introduction

To the victor go the spoils and nowhere is this truer than in the historic record. Many of the early British leaders are hidden in the mists of time; some, the ones who lost the crucial battles, have almost completely disappeared when the victors expunged their rivals from all extant records. The men—and a few women—who triumphed made sure that the records show their better claim to the throne, their better prowess in battle, and their greater magnanimity and consequently love and support of their peoples.

Sources for the early years of British history rely on fragments of information gathered from various charters, treaties, and ecclesiastical documents: the most notable of these for English history is the Anglo-Saxon Chronicle, a history of the Anglo-Saxons started in the late 9th century and copied, distributed, and recopied for the following 200 years or more. It is partial and not always correct, but it is an invaluable guide to the people and events that shaped early British history.

These early records are often the only source of information about various historical events, but they were often written sometime after the events described and are often based on hearsay; therefore, which bits are accurate and which bits are true leaves much room for historians to debate. Furthermore, only a few pieces of the original documents have survived the centuries, many of the records are copies of the original (if not copies of the copy) and so impossible to assess accurately for dating purposes. The truth of early historical events is often garnered through circumstantial evidence—mentions in city grants and church documents, even stray comments from

foreign observers, little is certain and much is debatable. Often the chroniclers have specific axes to grind—so Edwy All-Fair's reputation is besmirched by the chronicler of the life of St. Dunstan with whom the king argued.

Probably the most obvious and best known propagandist is the 16th-century playwright William Shakespeare, who needed the support of Queen Elizabeth I and the Tudor court to earn a living. Many of his plays reinforce the Tudor claim to the throne, which in truth was tenuous. His Tudor leanings are especially apparent with regard to King Richard who he portrayed as a murdering, evil tempered, crookback who was corrupt and unpopular with his subjects. These gross exaggerations and even outright lies were applauded by the Tudors and have largely passed down through history as facts. Such is the power of a great writer, as many a canny monarch has appreciated.

More recent historical events are not necessarily clearly documented and understood either; there is always somebody—often in power—who wants to hide or obscure the truth forcing historians to deduce true reasons behind events. An example of this is the Abdication Crisis in England in the 1930s.

Because of the paucity of reliable information from the early chronicles, many apparent "facts" are often little more than guesswork. Many of even the basic details of the earliest rulers are debatable: birth dates are rarely certain, spouses appear and disappear often for diplomatic reasons, and the numbers of children variable. This latter is understandable due to the very high mortality rate among infants and children until relatively recently. Additionally, life expectation was much shorter anyway, at a time when a king by definition led his men into battle, even an apparently minor wound could prove fatal through septacaemia or gangrene.

Kings were appointed by God and ruled in his name so it was a brave subject who went against the king. By and large unless a monarch was truly treacherous his subjects could be more or less guaranteed to support him against all comers. Even Charles

Above: Part of a late 13th century manuscript—known as Bodley Rolls 3—that shows the descent of Edward I from his mythological ancestor Brutus. Probably created as part of Edward's attempt to prove his claim on the Scottish throne. *The Art Archive/Bodleian Library Oxford AA395766*

I did not believe until the very last that his subjects would dare to execute him because his Divine Right overwhelmed all other claims. But in spite of this certainty of how power came to a monarch, the question of succession was always difficult.

In early Britain succession to the crown was not father to son (primogeniture) as it later became. Among the Anglo-Saxon kings it was from brother to brother; this way the monarch would often be an adult and considerably less risky than entrusting the kingdom to a child or young man. Inevitably such a pragmatic choice would lead to numerous rival claims, factions, and invading armies.

The early kings of Scotland were appointed through the law of tanistry that said that the crown should go to the best-qualified applicant. Inheritance originated from two lines of the House of Alpin that inevitably diverged over the years into two quite disparate rival families. This was legislated because in an age when a king had to prove his strength in battle, they almost inevitably failed to reach even middle age and so left as their heir a young boy who could not possibly hold his own against rival claimants nor protect the kingdom. Tanistry had the effect of giving the crown to the previous king's brother, or to the last but one king's son and so alternating from one line of the House of Alpin to the other. The system stopped in 954 with Máel Coluim mac Cináeda (Malcolm II) who took the precaution of making sure that all his rivals were murdered; many of the early kings of Scotland were murdered by their own followers or by rivals for their crown.

The British Isles comprise over six and a half thousand islands, so it is no surprise that early leaders used water as their primary means of transport at a time when most of the landscape was thickly covered with trees. The seas and rivers were ancient highways of trade and commerce as well as military conduits. This also explains why leaders in England saw no difficulty holding (and indeed claiming) lands in Scotland, Wales, Ireland, or even France and Denmark—and vice versa. National boundaries shape our modern views of history and we all see historical events through the viewpoint of individual countries, but for our ancestors such a demarcation is completely spurious.

It is misleading before more modern times to think of an "English," Scottish," or Welsh" king. Thanks to dynastic marriages and alliances, many rulers only notionally belonged to their country; most of them had foreign mothers and foreign wives and so produced mostly foreign children. Certainly in the case of England, the first few Norman kings and the first few Hanoverian kings did not speak or even understand English. The end result of all these marriages was that many of the ruling families of Europe were closely connected by blood and birth. Queen Victoria was an ancestor of virtually every ruling house in Europe at the the outbreak of World War I. The story of these complicated bloodlines is told in the following pages with reference to some—but not all—of Britain's monarchs. Where possible I have chosen those with the most interesting stories.

A note about spellings

For the purposes of this book we have used the modern anglicized forms of names—for example, Ethelbert rather than Aethelbert, Edward rather than Eadweard, and so on—and used their customary names.

Above: Coinage is always a good place to find a likeness of the monarch—in this case "By the Grace of God" Queen Elizabeth II on the obverse of a half crown piece. *The Art Archive/Alfredo Dagli Orti AA328397*

Right: A painting of Queen Elizabeth II by Scottish artist Sir William Oliphant Hutchison from 1956. She is wearing the robes of the Order of the Thistle. The modern order was founded by James VII of Scotland (James II of England). *The Art Archive/Co of Merchants, City of Edinburgh AA337146*

English Monarchy

The history of monarchy in England starts as the Roman hegemony over northwest Europe broke down. For nearly 400 years the Province of Britannia had seen Roman governors trying to maintain rule over an unruly island–something that required great walls and garrison towns filled with large numbers of troops. Roman Britain lost the direct support of Rome in the early part of the fifth century–some 50 or so years before the Western Roman Empire itself fell–and entered what we know as the "Dark Ages" that saw Germanic tribes invade Britain and push out its Celtic inhabitants.

As is usual whenever historians try to be black and white, there is much evidence to contradict this view: there were Saxon settlements in Britain as early as the fourth century; Roman organization and lifestyle continued on for some years after the empire left. However, what cannot be disputed is that after Roman troops left Britain, more and more barbarian attacks saw the arrival of the Angles (from whom we derive the name England), Saxons, Jutes and others. The British tribes fought the invaders–it is in this period that King Arthur is supposed to have lived–but were slowly overcome, and by the seventh century England was dominated by Anglo-Saxon kingdoms.

Between the seventh and ninth centuries England had many kingdoms: the so-called "Heptarchy" (from the Greek for seven and realm) refers to the kingdoms of East Anglia, Essex, Kent, Northumbria, Mercia, Sussex, and Wessex all of which developed in the period. Other kingdoms–such as the Jutes on the Isle of Wight–also flourished, but in the face of the next great danger to the country these smaller areas coalesced to provide a united front.

The Vikings first attacked England in the eighth century: by the middle of the ninth they had begun to settle the eastern coastal areas; and in 886 a treaty between Alfred the Great of Wessex and Danish Guthrum the Old formalized the partition of England between the English and the Vikings. By this time of the four greatest Anglo-Saxon kingdoms–East Anglia, Mercia, Northumbria, and Wessex–Wessex was the only one that had withstood the Danes, and it was from Wessex that today's monarchy stems. During the tenth century, the Danes were pushed out of the eastern counties and the Kingdom of England was established when King Edred finally took control of Northumbria in 954.

While England has remained England since that time, the fortunes of its monarchy have fluctuated dramatically. Within 50 years of Edred's death the Danes had conquered the whole of Britain. In 1016 the Danish Canute ruled England and Danish rule continued until 1042 when, following the death of Harthacanute, Edward the Confessor, Harthacanute's half-brother, succeeded him. The restored Anglo-

The history of the English monarchy after the arrival of the usurping Normans is well charted. From 1066 until the end of the 100 Years' War in the fifteenth century, England was part of a continental empire that stretched at times from the Pyrenees to Scotland. Thereafter confined to the British Isles, English monarchs took control of Wales (the Laws in Wales Acts of 1535–1542 created one kingdom of England and Wales); of Scotland (1707 Act of Union); and of Ireland (1801 Act of Union). It expanded its power over great swathes of the globe until, at its apogee in the 1920s, it ruled over a quarter of the world's population. During this time, the monarchy also changed: today's monarch is no longer an autocratic, absolute ruler whose power comes from God, and who holds the power of life and death over their subjects, but a constitutional monarch—a figurehead bound by laws and constitutions so that they have but nominal influence over the political life of the country.

The story of this thousand-year monarchy is recounted here through the reigns of most of the monarchs from Egbert of Wessex to Queen Elizabeth II, who is the constitutional monarch of the United Kingdom and Northern Ireland and the Commonwealth Realms.

Saxon monarchy lasted only a few months longer than its monarch.

Edward the Confessor died in 1066 and his brother-in-law Harold became king. Nine months later he lay dead on Senlac Hill and the duke of Normandy, William the Bastard, was monarch in his place.

Left: St. George's Cross was adopted by England as its national flag in the Middle Ages.

Egbert
House of Wessex
c. 769–839 (r. 802–839)

The son of Ealhmund of Kent and an unknown woman, Egbert was a descendant of Cerdic the founder of the kingdom of Wessex. As a rival to the throne of Wessex, Egbert was forced into exile in France in about 789 by Offa of Mercia and his son-in-law Beorhtric of Wessex. He lived at the court of the great Frankish King Charlemagne until the death of Beorhtric in 802, and he seems to have learned about the complexities of governing.

For the first 20 or so years little is known of Egbert's rule as king of Wessex but he seems to have managed to keep the kingdom independent from the aggressive King Offa of Mercia. In 815 he is recorded in the Anglo-Saxon Chronicle as ravaging the territories of the Dumnonia tribes in the west (now Cornwall).

In 825 Mercian domination of southern England was ended by defeat at the Battle of Ellendun (somewhere in Wiltshire), when it seems that Beornwulf of Mercia attacked the Wessex army. The Anglo-Saxon Chronicle gives an account of the battle and following events which are contradicted by other sources, but the upshot was that by the end of 825 Mercia had lost overlordship of lands in the southeast, particularly Kent, and the East Anglians also asked for protection from Wessex against the Mercians. When Beornwulf invaded Essex in response, he was killed (as was his

EGBERT.

successor), which allowed Egbert to invade Mercia in 829 and drive King Wiglaf into exile. From then on Egbert claimed to be king of Mercia and he is described as bretwalda or "wide ruler" (ie of all Britain). This was probably an overstatement of the facts but true in a very general way. Later that year the Anglo-Saxon Chronicle says that the Northumbrians submitted to Egbert, but other sources say he pillaged the lands there before they submitted. This was the height of Egbert's powers, although he is said to have been successful against the Welsh in 830.

Wiglaf, the exiled king of Mercia, successfully returned in 830 but did not manage to retain East Anglia; Egbert lost his control over southern England and possibly also of Essex and East Anglia. Historians conject that this was due to his loss of the foreign, Frankish, support which had won him initial power. Nevertheless, Egbert continued to control most of southeast England, incorporated the kingdoms of Sussex and Kent into Wessex, and retained control of Cornwall. His legacy was the domination of Wessex over southern England, the consolidation into Wessex of the southwest, and the permanent incorporation of Kent and Sussex into the kingdom.

Egbert died in 839 and was buried in Winchester. No records remain of a marriage but he did have legitimate children.

Left: Egbert, described as the "Ruler of Britain" in the *Anglo-Saxon Chronicle*, is portrayed here in *A History of England*. Thomas Babbington Macaulay's work was first published in 1849. *iStockphoto*

Ethelwulf
House of Wessex
c. 795–858 (r. 839–856)

While Egbert was still king of Wessex, his son Ethelwulf took his father's army to Kent where he conquered in his name: from then on he was known as the sub-king of Kent–and controlled lands which included Kent, Essex, Sussex, and Surrey. On the death of his father in 839, Ethelwulf was crowned at Kingston-upon-Thames. He became king of a Wessex that now incorporated the previously independent lands of Cornwall, Kent, and other parts of southeast England.

The details of his reign are sketchy and principally rely on the none-too reliable Anglo-Saxon Chronicle. Viking raids increased in both number and size and presented the greatest danger to the kingdom and to Britain as a whole; in 850 the Viking army wintered in England for the first time, on Thanet from where they stormed Canterbury and London. In 851 Ethelwulf, with his son Ethelbald beside him, defeated the Vikings in battle at Achleah in Surrey. The Anglo-Saxon Chronicle commented that there he oversaw "the greatest slaughter of a heathern army that was ever heard of to this present day."

Personally Ethelwulf is said to have been very religious, coupled with remarkably little political sense, although his greatest failure could be said to have fathered far too many sons– five, plus one daughter–with his wife Osburga, about whom very little is recorded. One of Ethelwulf's better

moves was to marry his daughter Ethelswith to Burghred, king of Mercia.

One of his first decisions on inheriting the throne was to split the kingdom: he kept the original Wessex lands (principally Wiltshire, Hampshire, Dorset, and Devon), and settled the newly acquired lands in the east–Kent, Sussex, Surrey, and Essex–to his eldest son Athelstan, who ruled there as sub-king.

Ethelwulf's piety instilled in him a great desire to make a pilgrimage to Rome: in 853 he sent his youngest son, Alfred (then about four years old) and joined him there in 855, the year after he was widowed. While in Rome he met Pope Benedict III and bestowed lavish riches on the clergy. On the return journey home Ethelwulf married Judith, the 12-year-old daughter of Charles the Bald, king of the western Franks and great-granddaughter of Charlemagne. They married at Verberie sur Oise in October 856. They had no issue, and she later married her stepson Ethelbald.

During Ethelwulf's absence Athelstan had died, and his next son– Ethelbald–was conspiring with the bishop of Sherborne and the ealdorman of Somerset to prevent his father from resuming the throne on his return, probably suspecting that Ethelwulf would make his youngest and favorite son Alfred his successor. But instead of plunging the country into civil war Ethelwulf did not contest Ethelbald's taking hold of Wessex and instead kept hold of Kent and the southeast himself. Ethelbald ruled there until his father's death, at age 62, on January 13, 858.

ETHELWOLF.

Initially buried at Steyning, he was then moved to the Old Minster in Winchester. By his will each of his surviving sons were to rule in turn so as to avoid young children inheriting the kingdom. In time the four youngest of Ethelwulf's five sons–Athelstan, Ethelbald, Ethelbert, Ethelred, and Alfred–succeeded to the throne.

Ethelbald
House of Wessex
c. 831–860 (r. 856–860)

Born the second son of King Ethelwulf of Wessex and his first wife Osburga, little is known about Ethelbald's early life except that in 850 he was given the rank of ealdorman and when he was in his early twenties he was left in charge of the western lands of Wessex–his brother Ethelburt was given charge of Kent–while his father went on pilgrimage to Rome in 855. While the king was away a coup was plotted to usurp the king. Ethelbald, if not in from the start, almost certainly joined the plot on hearing of his father's marriage to Judith, the young daughter of Charles the Bald.

From Ethelbald's point of view the danger was twofold: Ethelwulf could

father new rival sons (in fact he didn't) to threaten the succession of the throne, or may already have intended to leave his throne to his youngest and favorite son, Alfred (later to become Alfred the Great). Either way Ethelbald would be the loser. With the very real threat of civil war, the returning Ethelwulf conceeded the majority of Wessex to Ethelbald and retained only the southeast ern lands for himself. When Ethelwulf died in 858, Ethelbald inherited his entire kingdom with his younger brother becoming sub-king of Kent.

Ethelbald was crowned at Kingston-upon-Thames and soon scandalized many of his people and the church by marrying his stepmother, the 16-year-old

Above: Ethelburt (who reigned between 860 and 866) succeeded Ethelbald, his brother, as king of Wessex. Ethelburt was succeeded by another brother, Ethelred, who reigned until 871. *Ashmolean Museum via Jo St Mart*

Judith. Her father, Charles the Bald, was furious and forced his unlucky daughter into a nunnery at Senlis. The marriage was annulled in 860 on the grounds of consanguinity–in January 862 she eloped with Baldwin, Count of Flanders and became Countess of Flanders.

Ethelbald was only to reign for four years before dying, childless, in December 860 at the age of about 35, in Sherbourne, Dorset.

Ethelburt was the third son of King Ethelwulf of Wessex and Osburga. As with his older brothers who each in turn reigned before him, very little is known about him or his reign. When his brother Ethelbald was left in charge of the kingdom while their father went on pilgrimage to Rome, Ethelburt was given the lands of Kent to look after, which he probably retained as sub-king under his brother when he became king of Wessex. When Ethelbald died in 860

Above: Obverse of a silver penny minted during the reign of Ethelburt (Aethelberht). *Bridgeman Art Library/Getty Images 77011463*

Ethelburt became king in his turn and was also crowned at Kingston-upon-Thames on the coronation stone. Wessex was still suffering from regular Viking incursions, particularly in Northumbria and around the coast of Kent. In part due to these raids the newly amalgamated lands in the southeast became once and for all part of the kingdom of Wessex and, ultimately, England.

Ethelbert married and had two sons by a woman whose name has been lost in history; Aldhelm was killed during a Viking raid during his uncle Alfred's reign, and Ethelward, who claimed the throne in 899 on Alfred's death. He was rejected and had to flee to refuge in the Danelaw where he was killed in 900.

According to the Anglo-Saxon Chronicle, Ethelbert had been a good, peace-keeping king. He died in 866 and was buried at Sherbourne Abbey beside his brother Ethelbald; he was succeeded by his younger brother Ethelred.

Alfred the Great
House of Wessex
c. 849–899 (r. 871–899)

Born when the Vikings were threatening to overwhelm England, Alfred (or Aelfred) was the fifth son of the Aethelwulf, king of the West Saxons (Wessex). By 870, the year before he was born, the Vikings had overpowered the Anglo-Saxon kingdoms of Mercia and East Anglia and only Wessex remained independent. Alfred's elder brothers succeeded to the throne before him until in 871, at the age of 21, Alfred became king of Wessex on the death of his brother King Ethelred.

Alfred's first notable victory was at the Battle of Ashdown (871) in Berkshire when he led his brother's army and routed the Vikings. Nevertheless the Vikings resumed their victorious ways and by 878 had established their base at Chippenham in Wiltshire from where they set out to destroy the kingdom of Wessex. Alfred lost the following battles and while he refused to surrender, he did accept the necessity to pay regular tribute to keep the Danes at bay. With many of his people retreating to the Isle of Wight, Alfred and a few of his thegns disappeared into the Somerset tidal marshes to hide from the Vikings and have a base for their hit and run tactics. While there he is supposed to have been charged with watching a batch of cakes cooking; but preoccupied with battle plans, he neglected his task and the cakes burned. Perhaps it was then that he decided to build his own fortified base in the marshes at Athelney from where he summoned a new, highly mobile, army. Men arrived from across Wessex–from Somerset, Wiltshire, and Hampshire–and in May 878 together they defeated the Danes at the Battle of Edington, chasing the survivors back to their fortress at Chippenham where they were surrounded and surrendered 14 days later.

In the resulting Treaty of Wedmore Alfred made peace with the Danes and accepted the inevitability of them remaining in England. King Guthrum converted to Christianity and Alfred stood as his sponsor. By 886 Alfred had wrestled London from the Danish occupation and in a succeeding treaty England was partitioned using the Roman Watling Street as the east–west boundary. The Danes took eastern and northern England–the area became known as Danelaw, and by law English and Danes became equal–and Alfred took western and southern England including Kent and West Mercia.

To seal the bond, Alfred married Eahlswith, a Mercian noblewoman, and gave his daughter Aethrlflaed in marriage to the ealdorman of Mercia. Another daughter, Aelfthryth, was married to the Count of Flanders, a valuable ally and leader of a strong naval power.

From his new royal palace in Winchester Alfred considered how to cope with the constant threat of the Danes. He drew up his army consisting of the thegns (noblemen) and the fyrd (the militia)into a flexible rosta of militia who could rapidly respond to any

Right: This statue of Alfred the Great in Winchester was designed by Hamo Thornycroft, R.A., and erected in 1899.
via Jo St Mart

threats, yet not be away from their homes and farms for too long at a stretch. Additionally, Alfred reorganized the defenses of Wessex by starting a building program of well-defended burghs (fortified settlements) right across southern England; he strengthened the existing forts and constructed new as well. Peasant settlers were given land on condition they manned the defenses when required, and none were more than 20 miles from the safety of a burgh. The details of these grants and fortifications were recorded in the Burghal Hidage. Additionally, Alfred ordered the building of first English navy, consisting of big, fast new ships which would defend the southern coastline of England against the raiding Danes. In other areas Alfred encouraged the learning of Latin (he even learned it himself and translated books into English) and was the patron of the Anglo-Saxon Chronicle, the contemporary history of the English people. He also established justice across his lands through the use of a legal code assembled from the best laws of earlier rulers, particularly Offa of Mercia, then adding his own legal strictures to produce a definitive Anglo-Saxon law. He reformed the coinage and allowed their minting in his new burhs; on these he was known as the king of the English (not just Wessex).

Alfred died aged 50 on October 26, 899, and was buried in Winchester. The first true king of the English, Alfred the Great was the first ruler to unite the majority of his people under one rule and set up the legal and military establishments to protect them against a dangerous and strong enemy.

Edward (Eadweard) the Elder

House of Wessex
c. 872–924 (r. 899–924)

The oldest surviving son of Alfred the Great and Ealhswith, Edward was born sometime between 874 and 877 and became king on his father's death in 899. In time he proved to be a shrewd and able strategist and a very capable administrator who laid many of the foundations for a united and cohesive kingdom from his capital in Winchester. By the end of his reign the separate kingdoms of Wessex and Mercia had united to form the basis of the future kingdom of England.

According to Asser (Bishop of Sherborne and biographer of King Alfred), Edward was educated at court alongside his younger sister Elfthryth (who later married the Count of Flanders). Although known as the king's son, filius regis–the heir–Edward was not his father's obvious successor. By Anglo-Saxon precedent the two sons of King Ethelred (his father's older brother) had a stronger claim to the throne: Aethelwold and Aethelhelm were about ten years older and more experienced, plus their mother had been crowned queen, which Edward's mother had not.

Edward first emerges from childhood in the historic record in 893 when,

leading his father's army, he was victorious against a large raiding Danish army at Farnham in Surrey. This experience undoubtedly helped him when his cousin Aethelwold made a bid for the crown (there is no record of Aethelhelm, so he was probably already dead) in 899 by seizing Wimborne in Dorset, and then Christchurch. In reply Edward marched his army to nearby Badbury but Ethelwold would not give battle and instead fled one night to Northumbria where the Danes proclaimed him king in Jorvik.

On June 8, 900, Edward was crowned on the coronation stone in Kingston-upon-Thames. The next year in the fall, Aethelwold and his Viking fleet arrived in Essex looking for and getting the support of the East Anglian Danes in his bid to take the crown of Wesex. In 902 Edward and his Wessex army met Aethelwold and his Northumberland Danes in battle at Holme in Essex. The battle was largely indecisive except that both Aethelwold and the Danish king Eohric of Northumberland lost their lives; so, not only had Edward eliminated his rival for the throne but also removed one of the most dangerous Viking leaders.

Between 909 and 920 Edward set about extending and uniting his kingdom against the Danes with the assistance of a strong, militarily capable, and loyal ally, his older sister Ethelflaed, the wife of Ethelred, ealdorman of Mercia, after whose death in 911 became known as the Lady of the Mercians.

First Edward made peace with the East Anglians and then in 909 he sent an army north to attack Northumbria. In return the Danes attacked Mercia and on

August 5, 910, the two sides met at the Battle of Tettenhall (in Staffordshire). The allied forces of Mercia under the command of Ethelred of Mercia and Wessex had a decisive victory over the Northumbrian Vikings, although Ethelred died there. This battle has gone down in history as the defeat of the last great Viking army to ravage England; the Danes never again posed a real threat to the kingdom and never again raided south of the Humber. Moreover, following this victory Wessex and Mercia were now more united than ever. To make sure the Danes stayed in the north, Edward and his sister built a series of 28 fortresses (or burhs) as civilian and military strongpoints in strategically crucial positions across the width of the northern lands.

As his reign progressed Edward consolidated his hold over Mercia, East Anglia, and Essex taking over and conquering the formerly Danish-held lands (the southern Danelaw) and taking control of the important cities of London and Oxford. In 918 Ethelflaed died leaving her daughter Aelfwynn as her successor, but Edward moved quickly to take all her Mercian holdings into his own hands; this may not have been so peaceable and easy as contemporary records suggest. Wessex laws and administration were imposed over the lands and new shires created.

By that same year all the Danes living south of the River Humber had submitted to Edward and, according to the Anglo-Saxon Chronicle, by the time he died even the Danish king of York, the Anglian Lord of Bamburgh, the King of the Britons of Strathclyde, and the King of Scots had acknowledged Edward as "Father and lord."

Edward died on July 17, 924, at the age of about 50 while leading his army against a Welsh-Mercian rebellion at Farndon-upon-Dee in Cheshire. His body was taken back south for burial at Winchester. Over the course of his life Edward had married three times and fathered about 14 legitimate children. He was briefly succeeded by his son Elfward.

Elfward (Aelfweard)
House of Wessex
c. 903–924 (r. July 18–August 2, 924)

Elfward was King of Wessex for 15 days but not a great deal else is known about him except that he was the second son of Edward The Elder and his second wife Queen Aelfflaed. It is even possible that he was a hermit living in Bridgnorth, Staffordshire at the time of his father's death. He was proclaimed by the men of Wessex as their king on the death of his father on July 17, 924, at the same time as his older half-brother Athelstan was proclaimed king of Mercia by the Mercians in Gloucester. (The legitimate successor to Mercia, Aelfwynn, had–thanks to Edward–disappeared in Wessex somewhere, probably into a nunnery.) But Elfward died suddenly, cause unknown, in Oxford on August 2, 924, before his coronation: this may well have been perpetrated by Athelstan or some of his supporters. He was buried beside his father Edward in the New Minster at Winchester and his half-brother Athelstan became king of both Wessex and Mercia.

Athelstan the Glorious
House of Wessex
c. 895–939 (r. 925–939)

Alfred the Great's grandson, and son of King Edward the Elder, Athelstan became the first king of all England through his military leadership. In the north this was achieved through ejecting the Danes from the city of York in 927, and in the south by taking control of Cornwall. Neighboring rulers such as the north British kings (ie Welsh kings), and King Constantine II of Scotland were forced to submit to him as "father and lord"; Constantine at the Treaty of Eamont Bridge in 927, and the Welsh following submission at Hereford when they were they had to agree to paying enormous annual tribute– sources indicate this included 25,000 oxen annually. In 937 many of these opponents united under the leadership of the king of Scotland and with help from Olaf of Dublin, attempted an invasion of England which Athelstan repelled with an army drawn from across the land with a decisive victory at the Battle of Brunanburgh in 937.

Athelstan increased his control over the kingdom by improving the law codes and regulating the silver currency to

Left: The elevation of Edward the Elder at his coronation, Kingston-upon-Thames, 900. *Popperfoto/Getty Images 78952142*

Right: Athelstan as seen in a capital of an illuminated version of the *Anglo-Saxon Chronicle. History Department, UCL via Jo St. Mart*

limit fraud. Across central England the shire system was established and the growth of town life encouraged. He also established important dynastic ties with western rulers by marrying off four of his half sisters to important noble allies— in Scandinavia, Saxony, and Brittany.

Personally Athelstan was a deeply religious man and a great collector and giver of religious works of art and relics. He worked hard to gain the support of the church for his rule. He died on October 27, 939, and was buried in his favorite Malmesbury Abbey where his tomb can still be seen. He died childless and was succeeded by his 18-year-old half-brother Edmund.

Below: Edmund the Magnificent from *A History of England. iStockphoto*

Edmund the Magnificent
House of Wessex
c. 921–946 (r. 939–946)

Son of Edward the Elder, and his third wife, Edgith, Edmund succeeded his half-brother Athelstan to the throne in 939 at the age of 18. He had not been on the throne for long before he was challenged: first King Olaf Guthfrithson of Dublin returned to northern England–he had been defeated at the Battle of Brunanburgh in 937 by Athelstan and the young Edmund but two years later in 939 occupied York, probably by invitation of the Northumbrians, before moving south to raid the midlands of England. Edmund marched his army north where he besieged Olaf and Archbishop Wulfstan of York in Leicester. After much negotiation between the latter and Archbishop Oda of Canterbury a peace treaty was agreed in 940. The resulting treaty forced Edmund to cede the lands of northeast Mercia between Watling Street and the River Humber, to Olaf, King of York (lands only recently conquered by King Edward in 918–20).

A few years later in 941 Olaf was killed while out raiding in Northumbria and was replaced by his cousin Olaf Sihtricson (or Sigtryggson). Edmund seized the opportunity and moved north again and reconquered the lost territories of the Five Boroughs of the East Midlands. This time, in 943, Olaf Sihtricson was the loser and on making peace was baptized a Christian with Edmund standing as his godfather. Edmund then turned to crush the

opportunistic Welsh revolt of King Idwal of Gwynedd.

In 944 Ragnall Guthfrithson challenged Olaf for the throne of York but Edmund was now strong enough to take York himself, expel the rivals, and take control of Northumbria himself. Olaf was ousted from his throne and fled to Dublin. He became king of Dublin but remained Edmund's ally. Back in the north in 945 Edmund consolidated his latest conquest by ravaging the British kingdom of Strathclyde and killing King Donald MacDonald, but rather than occupying the country he signed a mutual treaty of military support by land and sea with the new overlord, Malcolm I and conceded his rights over the lands there. This was the first treaty between England and Scotland that established the borders of Anglo-Saxon England and ensured that the borders of the two countries would thenceforward be peaceful.

It was during this period of relative calm that the monastaries began a revival across England helped by the mutual support between the crown and Archbishop Oda. Edmund took the opportunity provided by peace to reorganize the coinage and issue two new law codes.

Edmund married twice: his first wife, Elgiva (later St. Elgiva), gave him sons Edwy and Edgar. When she died in 944 he married Aethelflaed, but they had no children.

Right: Edmund the Magnificent, who acceded to the throne in 939. He would die seven years later at the tender age of 25. *History Department, UCL via Jo St. Mart*

His death came unexpectedly: on May 26, 946, at the age of about 25 Edmund was present at a party in his royal villa at Pucklechurch, Gloucestershire when he spotted Leofa, an outlawed thief in the crowd. The latter was ordered to leave and when he refused a fight broke out between Leofa and a steward–it seems that when Edmund tried to intervene he was fatally stabbed in the stomach by Leofa and died almost instantly; Leofa was then himself killed.

Edmund was buried at Glastonbury where he had only recently appointed Dunstan (later St. Dunstan) as abbot.

Edred

House of Wessex
c. 923–955 (r. 946–955)

Edred was the son of king Edward the Elder and his third wife, Edgiva, daughter of Sigehelm, Ealdorman of Kent. Following the murder of his older brother Edmund I in 946, Edred, who was about the age of 21, was chosen to be king by the Witan, instead of Edmund's two sons Edwy and Edgar who were too young. This was an era of political infidelity and allegiances changed quickly according to prevailing circumstances. Initially supported by oaths of fidelity from the Northumbrian ealdormen at Tanshief in Yorkshire, many of his northern people changed their allegiance within the year to support Eric Bloodaxe, the Viking king of York. In 948 Edred took his army to

Ripon where he burnt the minster before moving out and off into the countryside laying waste to the land. His army was attacked by angry Northerners at Castleford; in response Edred returned to Northumbria and pillaged the land again, convincing many of Eric Bloodaxe's supporters to return to Edred's side.

In the late 950 the Northerners revolted again and appealed to Olaf Sihtricsson to be their leader but within two years swapped allegiance again back to Eric Bloodaxe. He, too, was abandoned in 954 by his fickle supporters who returned to pledge their allegiance to Edred. Eric Bloodaxe left York and England for good.

Although a proven and successful soldier who battled the Vikings many times, Edred suffered from poor health. He was reportedly small and never very strong although a brave soldier: at times he could hardly eat thanks to a persistent and unidentified stomach problem.

After ruling for almost nine and a half years he died of his mystery stomach ailment on November 23, 955, at his palace in Frome in Somerset. He was somewhere in his thirties. Against his wishes he was buried alongside his ancestors in Winchester cathedral. Unmarried, he had brought up his brother Edmund's sons Edwy and Edgar as his own and each succeeded to the crown in turn.

Left: Victorian image of Edred, King of Wessex, as taken from *A History of England*. Edred died in Frome in Somerset in 955. *iStockphoto*

Edwy All-Fair

House of Wessex
c. 941–959 (r. 955–959)

Aged somewhere between 13 and 16 years old, Edwy (also known as Edwig) succeeded his uncle, King Edred, to the throne of England in 955. He was crowned by Archbishop Odo at Kingston-upon-Thames on the border between Anglo-Saxon England and the Danelaw and on the Wessex-Mercia border. Brought up by his uncle, Edwy was the eldest son of King Edmund (the Magnificent) and Elgiva.

At his coronation feast he fell foul of Archbishop Odo and Dunstan (later Saint Dunstan), Abbot of Glastonbury, to such an extent that Dunstan went into exile and would not return until Edwy's death.

There are few sources for a detailed examination of Edwy's reign–and the main one (a life of St. Dunstan) was, of course, written by someone who was in inimicable to him. Our view of Edwy is, therefore, jaundiced.

In 957 the thanes of Mercia and Northumbria–feeling, it is said, sidelined by the lavishness disposed on Wessex, and supported by Edwy's enemy, Archbishop Odo–switched their allegiance to Edwy's brother Edgar. Civil war threatened and the two sides met in battle at Gloucester with Edwy the loser.

Right: Another Victorian image—king of England from 955 to 959, Edwy's reign was troubled with conflict with his brother Edgar. *iStockphoto*

E D W Y.

Rather than risk all-out civil war, the nobility agreed to a partition of the country with the River Thames as the boundary. Edwy retainied the south (Wessex and Kent) and Edgar took everything to the north. The dispute largely settled, Edwy was able to rule–"more wisely" the chronicler tells us–supporting the church, and granting many gifts and charters.

Edwy died young–at age 18 or 19–and was buried in Winchester cathedral beside his ancestors. His throne was taken by his brother Edgar who reunited the kingdom.

Edgar the Peaceful (or Peaceable)

House of Wessex
c. 943–975 (r. 959–975)

The youngest child of King Edmund and St. Aelfgith, Edgar was orphaned by the time he was three: his mother died within a year of bearing him and his father was murdered two years later. After much discussion, Edmund was fostered in the household of the most powerful noble in the country–Athelstan Half-King, Ealdorman of East Anglia–and his wife Aelfwinn. Athelstan was an enthusiastic supporter of monastic reform and ensured that his young charge was tutored by the Benedictine monk St. Aethelwold, Abbot of Abingdon; this strongly religious upbringing was to greatly influence his decisions and lifestyle.

In 955 Edgar's 14-year-old brother Edwy became king on the death of their

uncle, King Edred. Two years later the northern thegns of Mercia lost faith in their monarch and switched their allegiance to Edgar making him king of the north in preference to the Edwy, who was in conflict with the other great power in the land, the church.

In 958 with the support of the nobility England was divided–Edwy retained Wessex and Edgar (now 14 years old) took the northern lands of Mercia and Northumbria. To advise and support him Edgar immediately recalled Dunstan from exile (imposed by Edwy) and made him Bishop of Worcester (957), and then London (959). Dunstan remained Edgar's chief advisor throughout his reign.

In October 959 Edwy died leaving Edgar King of England at the age of 16, he was initially crowned at Kingston-upon-Thames and then again in a bigger, more formal, ceremony at Bath in 973 where he was declared King of the English.

One of his first moves was to appoint Dunstan Archbishop Canterbury (in 961) and in the process push forward the monastic reform movement. Both Edgar and Dunstan were determined to reform the great monastic houses and clean up their lax way of life by imposing the austere monastic discipline of St. Benedictine. Old monasteries were cleaned up and about 40 new Benedictine monasteries were founded across the kingdom with accompanying grants of huge areas of land and legal support, such as making the payment of tithes to the church compulsory; few of these moves were popular with the general populace but together the church and monarchy reinforced and supported each other.

After his second coronation Edgar assembled a great army and marched them north to Chester where the kings of the north (the sources vary on numbers but they included King Kenneth of the Scots, Malcolm of Strathclyde and Cumbria, King Maccus of Man and the Western Isles, Iago of Gwynedd, and possibly also King Idwallon of Morgannwg, and King Sigefrith) all came and pledged their loyalty and submission. Edgar's reign is characterized by being comparatively peaceful as he benefitted from the political unity of the kingdom instead of the numerous rival kingships of earlier Britain; in his own words, he ruled for "all the nations, whether Englishmen, Danes or Britons."

One of the most significant actions of Edgar's reign was the reform of the coinage: in 973 all coins in circulation were called back to the 40 or so mint towns where they were reminted with a new design. This regulated the coinage and reinforced his image among his countrymen.

Edgar died on July 8, 975, aged 32 and was buried in St. Dunstan's Abbey, Glastonbury where he was soon prayed to as a saint. He had been a popular, peacetime monarch and the first king to rule all three of the major kingdoms of Northumbria, Mercia, and Wessex. Additionally, Edgar is credited with reorganizing the English fleet, which sources say circumnavigated Britain every year in a show of might and power. The only major blot on his character is his liason with Wulfthryth, a nun who bore him a daughter, Eadgyth (both in time became abbesses and saints). Edgar left three sons from his two wives; from Ethelflaed a boy later known as Edward the Martyr, and from Aelfthryth two sons, Aetheling Edmund (who died young) and Ethelred the Unready. For almost a hundred years until the Norman Conquest every succession to the throne of England was strenuously contested.

Right: Edward the Martyr died at the hands of an assassin near Corfe Castle (shown here). After miracles took place at his tomb in Shaftesbury Abbey, he was sanctified. After the Reformation his remains were hidden and now reside in relics in a church in Brookwood Cemetery, in Woking. *iStockphoto*

Edward the Martyr
House of Wessex
c. 962–978 (r. 975–978)

Edward was the oldest son of King Egdar and his first wife Ethelflaed–although possibly of his mistress Wulfthryth. He was in his early teens when his father died. The succession to the throne was disputed by supporters of his half-brother Ethelred (aged around seven), but Edward was supported by the Witan, Oswald of Worcester the Archbishop of York, and Dunstan, Archbishop of Canterbury (later St. Dunstan), who crowned him.

At the time of Edward's accession to the throne, famine was stalking the kingdom and antimonastic feelings were running high. In Mercia, in particular, many monasteries were destroyed and monks thrown off the land. Edward was devout and enjoyed handing large endowments of land and money to churches and monasteries, much to the outrage of the local ealdormen and thegns. This caused animosity among the populace in general, who resented the affluent clergy at a time when they were starving and struggling.

Outside the church Edward's unpopularity grew in the three short years of his reign with his own violent outbursts of rage often offending important people.

Three years into his reign on March 18, 978, Edward was out hunting with horses and dogs in Dorset around Wareham and near his half-brother's lands at Corfe Castle. Apparently on impulse he decided to visit his brother, left his retinue behind and arrived at the castle alone. Contemporary monastic writers recorded that Ethelred's retainers surrounded Edward and stabbed him while still on his horse. It was rumored a century later that his stepmother handed a glass of mead while one of her retinue stabbed him: nobody was punished for the atrocity. Aged somewhere between 10 and 13 years old, Ethelred was crowned within a month.

Edward's legacy was promoted by the church (who had lost a more than generous sponsor) and he was soon spoken of as a saint and a cult site was established at Shaftesbury Abbey where his bones were brought from his original hasty burial site at Wareham.

Above: Ethelred's troops in battle against Sweyn I of Denmark. In 1013 Sweyn conquered the country but his success was short-lived. He died five weeks later. *History Department, UCL via Jo St. Mart*

Right : A coin from the reign of Ethelred the Unready. *History Department, UCL via Jo St. Mart*

Ethelred the Unready (or Redeless)

House of Wessex
c. 968–1016 (r. 979–1016)

Ethelred was the son of Edgar the Peaceable and his second wife Elfrida, and became king at about the age of 13 on the death of his half-brother Edward the Martyr, who was murdered by Ethelred's followers in 978, including, perhaps, his own ambitious mother Queen Elfrida; he was too young to be implicated in the plot. Ethelred's nickname "Unready" (or Redeless) means that he was without wise counsel–which he needed at such an early age.

Indeed he was unable to gather effective political support from among the nobility or commoners and the church, in particular, opposed his rule and worked to turn Edward into a martyr.

In 980 initially small-scale Viking raids resumed (in 980, 981, 982, and 988); the Danes were allies (and distant relatives) of the Normans and so supported each other diplomatically causing increased tension between England and Normandy. For the sake of harmony, Pope John XV drew up a peace treaty between the two which was ratified in Rouen in 991. But that same year a massive Viking raid into England culminated in the Battle of Maldon and a crushing defeat for the brave thegns of Essex. To stop such an atrocity happening again, Ethelred agreed to pay the Danish demand for tribute, some 10,000 pounds, which would guarantee the peace. However, it did not stop the raids: in 994 a huge Danish fleet arrived in London where an uneasy treaty was agreed: 22,000 pounds of gold and silver were handed to the Danes to ensure the peace. This tribute became known as Danegeld, but did not stop the raiding, with the Viking fleet using the Isle of Wight as a base. A truce was bought again in 1002 at the cost of 24,000 pounds, but only brought temporary respite. Danish armies continued to arrive and ravage England from north to south and east to west, with Danegeld paid at the culmination of each attack, and each larger than the last. By 1012, 48,000 pounds weight of silver was handed over to the Danes in London.

Ethelred was not a fighting king and relied on Danegeld and diplomacy for the safety of his kingdom. Following the Peace of Rouen in 991, he maintained a diplomatic alliance with the powerful and ambitious Duke of Normandy, and later married his daughter Emma–so establishing the somewhat tenuous claim to the English throne for William, Duke of Normandy almost 70 years later. Emma herself and her retinue of Normans were generally unpopular and increased Ethelred's already low personal popularity.

Hatred and fear of the Danes and the demands of the Danegeld tax reached such a pitch that on November 18, 1002 (St. Brice's Day), Ethelred ordered the massacre of all the Danes in England; one of the slain was Gunhilda, sister of Sweyn Forkbeard, the king of Denmark, and he swore to avenge his sister. Accordingly in 1013 Sweyn and his army invaded England causing a terrified Ethelred and his wife to flee to Normandy to take refuge with her family. But Sweyn unexpectedly died five weeks later of an apoplexy while investing Bury St. Edmunds, and the hastily gathered Witan instead of supporting the claim of Canute invited Ethelred to return to his throne. Initially joyously received, Ethelred soon alienated his followers again and they were not sorry when he died in London in 1016 with Canute at the gates of the city. Ethelred was buried at old St. Paul's cathedral, and his queen Emma soon after married King Canute.

Ethelred's legacy was to leave a complicated succession to the throne by fathering many children: first with Aelgifu, the daughter of Thored, Ealdorman of Northumbria he had six sons including Edmund Ironside and four daughters; His second wife (m. 1002) was Duke Richard II of Normandy's sister, Emma of Normandy and together they had two sons (Edward the Confessor and Alfred) and a daughter.

Edmund Ironside
House of Wessex
c. 990–1016 (r. April 24–November 30, 1016)

Edmund gained his nickname "Ironside" for the way he repelled the Danish Viking invasion led by King Canute. He was born somewhere in Wessex, the second son of Ethelred the Unready and his first wife, Aelfgifu of Northumbria. As a young prince of Wessex he fought bravely–but ultimately without success–against the invading Danes led by Canute. He succeeded as the designated heir to his older brother Athelstan in 1014, but his father King Ethelred wanted Athelstan's holdings for himself. To weaken his son's position the king had two of his principal allies–Danish earls Sigeferth and Morcar–executed, but Edmund retaliated by strengthening his claim by marrying Aeldgyth (Edith), Sigeferth's widow, who had been confined to a nunnery. Edmund then moved to the Five Boroughs (Stamford, Leicester, Lincoln, Nottingham, and Derby) were the people all submitted to him.

While all this family infighting was going on, the ambitious King Canute seized the opportunity to invade England with his armies that summer.

In spring 1015 Edmund openly rebelled against his father–possibly because he feared being passed over for his half-brothers Edward and Alfred in the succession to the throne–by allying with Earl Utred of Northumbria, and then devastated much of northwest Mercia; however, the earl proved unreliable and quickly pledged his support for Canute instead–in due course Canute repaid Utred by having him murdered. Left without support, Edmund reconciled with his desperately ill father who was lying sick in London.

Ethelred did not recover from his illness and died on April 23, 1016, at a time when Canute was proving his strength in England and was surrounding the city of London. Handed the reigns of power by the people of London, Edmund was crowned King of England at St. Paul's Cathedral on April 14, 1016. He bravely attempted to defend his inheritance, but the Witan in Southampton chose Canute as their king. As the Danes besieged London, Edmund made haste for Wessex to raise an army to repel the invaders: when the Englishmen stood and fought the Danes were driven back. Successful in battle, the Wessex army moved to raise the Danish siege of London and then proceeded to repeatedly beat the Danes five times in battle. In the sixth battle, at Ashington (or Assandun) in Essex on October 18, Canute scored a decisive victory thanks to the treachery of Edric Streona, an aeldorman of the Mercians and Edmund's brother-in-law. The English were betrayed and then slaughtered, but Edmund escaped although wounded, to Gloucestershire. He was reluctantly pressured into agreeing a peace through lack of support from the Witan. At the resulting Treaty of Olney (October 1016) Edmund and

Canute swore friendship and divided the kingdom. Legend says that Edmund invited Canute to single combat to limit the loss of life, but Canute declined on the grounds that the fight would be unfair because Edmund was so much bigger and stronger. Instead they negotiated a peace treaty on an island in the middle of the River Severn in Gloucestershire. This resulted in Edmund retaining Essex, and Canute taking all the lands north of the River Thames including the important city of London. But the crucial clause was their pledge that whoever of them died first, the other would inherit their territories.

On November 30, 1016, King Edmund died suddenly at about the age of 26. He had been king of England for only eight months and left Canute as sole king of England. The cause of death is unknown: it was probably from wounds sustained in battle, but could also have been through treachery. Edmund Ironside was buried at Glastonbury Abbey in Somerset; his tomb was destroyed and lost during the Dissolution of the Monasteries in the mid-16th century. With his wife Aeldgyth of East Anglia he had fathered two children, Edward and Edmund. The boys were gathered up by King Canute and sent to Sweden where they were supposed to be quietly despatched; instead they were sent to Kievan Russia and then on to Hungary.

Viking Canute was left the undisputed king of England and his accession ushered in a reign of stability and prosperity.

Canute

House of Denmark
c. 990–1035 (r. 1016–1035)

After a battle-strewn start, King Canute became a successful leader who turned England into a stable and prosperous land. Once his rule was established, in 1027 Canute claimed to be the "King of all England and Denmark and the Norwegians and of some of the Swedes" and at various times extended his reign to various (now Scottish) islands, parts of mainland Scotland, the Isle of Man, and Dublin.

Son of Danish King Sweyn Forkbeard and an unknown mother, Canute's birth date and place are also a mystery, and little is recorded until he accompanied his father on his successful invasion of England in summer 1013. As the Viking raiders marched inland, Canute was left in command of the fleet at Gainsborough. In February 1014 Forkbeard died suddenly leaving Canute as his heir to England and his eldest son Harald as king of Denmark. However, the English nobility did not want to accept him and at the Witan (high council) they voted for the return of the exiled Anglo-Saxon King Ethelred the Unready from Normandy, where he was living with his in-laws. Canute left for Denmark where he prepared for an even bigger invasion of England.

Left: King Canute as seen on Bodley Rolls 3, traditionally part of Edward I's case for claiming Scotland after the death of Margaret, the Maid of Norway.
The Art Archive/ Bodleian Library Oxford AA395766

Canute returned with 200 longships and a Viking army of 10,000 men in summer 1015. He had the support of many European (mostly Scandinavian) allies and, crucially, the Earl of Mercia, Eadric Streona, probably the richest English nobleman. The Viking fleet quickly sailed down the east coast of England, through the English Channel, around the Cornish peninsula, and then up the Bristol Channel all the way to Bristol from were they landed and invaded inland into the heart of Wessex. This attack caught the English by surprise and Ethelred was forced to retreat to London as his country was invaded and conquered. Besieged in London, Ethelred died there in April 1016 leaving his son Edmund Ironside king.

Fortunes ebbed and flowed on both sides until eventually the decisive Battle of Ashingdon in October 1016 in which Canute finally triumphed. Edmund was cornered in Gloucestershire and agreed the Treaty of Olney which conceded all of England except Wessex to Canute. Crucially they also agreed that whichever of them outlived the other would become sole king of England, as would his heirs. Accordingly, when Edmund died on November 30 Canute became undisputed king of England.

The following summer, in July 1017, Canute married Emma—Ethelred's widow and daughter of the Duke of Normandy. Their son, Harthacanute, was declared heir to the

throne rather than Canute's previous sons by an earlier marriage, or Ethelred and Emma's two exiled sons. Harthacanute was sent to Denmark where he was brought up as a Viking prince.

The most famous story about King Canute concerns the sea. Many of his fawning courtiers eulogized Canute, claiming he could do anything. In frustration and to prove his fallibility he ordered his throne set up on the beach at Bosham from where he commanded the waves. "Go back, sea." But the sea still advanced and his feet got wet but he had made his point to his followers and is quoted as saying, "Let all men know how empty and worthless is the power of kings. For there is none worthy of the name but God, whom heaven, earth, and sea obey."

Constitutionally Canute divided England into four great earldoms: Wessex, Mercia, East Anglia, and Northumbria. He also revived many of the earlier English laws to establish order and justice across the land and ordered that the coinage be aligned with that of Denmark to the benefit of trade and governance of both countries. Viking raiders stopped attacking England allowing the country an unprecedented era of stability and prosperity. The last Danegeld–82,500 pounds–was paid to Canute in 1018, and much of his Viking army was allowed to return home to Scandinavia with a handsome payoff. Canute respected and upheld the teachings of the church which, in turn, supported him. He repaired the damaged churches and monasteries and built new ones. He even journeyed to Rome (1027–1028) to meet the pope and be present at the coronation of the new Holy Roman Emperor (Conrad II) whom he stood beside as an equal.

In 1018 Canute's brother, Harald of Denmark, died and Canute traveled to Denmark to claim the throne. While abroad Canute used trusted and powerful earls to run the government. In 1028 Canute took a fleet of 50 ships to conquered Norway where he was crowned king in Trondheim.

Canute died in Shaftesbury, Dorset in November 1035, aged about 40 and was buried in Winchester.

Left: King Canute and Queen Emma. Canute's second wife, Emma of Normandy was the widow of Ethelred the Unready. *History Department, UCL via Jo St. Mart*

Above right: Harold Harefoot. *The Art Archive/Bodleian Library Oxford*

Harold Harefoot
House of Denmark
c. 1015–1040 (r. 1035–1040)

Son of King Canute and Aelgifu of Northampton, Harold temporarily became regent of England with Emma of Normandy (Harthacanute's mother) in 1035 to represent his younger half-brother, as the latter was embroiled in repelling invaders in Denmark. Harold became king of England in 1037 by popular acclaim when Emma fled to Flanders, and he was crowned at Oxford. A year earlier Alfred Atheling and his brother Edward (later the Confessor) returned from Normandy ostensibly to visit their mother Emma in Winchester. Suspicious of their motives, Harold had Alfred captured and blinded; he died soon after of his wounds. Harold died aged 24 in March 1040 after ruling for four years and 16 weeks, just as Harthacanute's invasion fleet was on its way to England.

Right: Victorian image of Edmund Ironside, King of Wessex, as taken from *A History of England. iStockphoto*

Harthacanute

House of Denmark
c. 1018–1042 (r. 1040–1042)

Son of King Canute and his second wife Emma of Normandy, Harthacanute was his father's designated heir in Denmark and England, but was supplanted in England by his half-brother Harold Harefoot for four years until the latter died. Harthacanute's invasion force of 62 warships was en route for England when Harold Harefoot died, so Harthacanute was accepted as king uncontested. After his coronation at Canterbury he had Harold's body violated and flung into a marsh, and imposed the punitive "fleet tax" (to pay for his invasion costs) on the English for accepting Harold as their king. A very unpopular monarch, Harthacanute died aged 24 during a drinking session after a wedding feast in Lambeth.

Above: King Harthacanute from the Bodley Rolls 3. *The Art Archive/Bodleian Library Oxford AA395766*

Edward the Confessor
House of Wessex
c. 1003–1066 (r. 1042–1066)

The penultimate Anglo-Saxon king of England was unable to unite his kingdom behind him thanks to his perceived favoritism towards his Norman advisors. This unpopularity allowed the wealth and strength of three powerful earls, Godwin, Earl of Wessex, Leofric, Earl of Mercia, and Siward, Earl of Northumbria to grow. Accordingly, when Edward died without producing an heir, the kingdom was left prey to powerful and ambitious suitors.

Edward was the youngest son of Ethelred the Unready and Emma of Normandy, but following the Danish invasion of England by Canute in 1013 he and his brother Alfred were sent to live with their Norman cousins. There the harsh childhood and strict religious upbringing influenced his life. Edward was recalled to England by his half-brother Harthacanute, the new king in 1041, and in turn took the throne when Hardicanute died in 1042, allegedly following a serious drinking session.

In April 1043 Edward was crowned in Winchester cathedral as the new king to popular acclaim. The Anglo-Saxon Chronicle states that one of his first decisions was to remove all his mother's estates so reducing her to relative poverty in retaliation for the miserable

Left: St. Edward the Confessor celebrates Easter 1053. Bottom right, the death of Godwin in 1053. *History Department, UCL via Jo St. Mart*

childhood she endorsed–that and her support for Magnus I of Norway for the throne of England.

For diplomatic reasons Edward married Edith, daughter of Godwin of Wessex, the most powerful nobleman in the land; crucially the marriage proved childless. Some years later in 1051 a number of important Normans were killed during a fight in the port of Dover; anxious to placate his powerful Norman relatives and allies, Edward ordered his father-in-law Earl Godwin to punish the people of Dover. Godwin refused and instead gathered an army to oppose Edward. But the earls of Mercia and Northumbria remained loyal to Edward, so Godwin fled to his relatives in Flanders instead.

Edward chose to surround himself with Norman courtiers and advisors much to the annoyance of the Anglo-Saxon nobility. This unpopularity encouraged Earl Godwin to gather an invading army commanded by his sons Tostig and Harold, and return to England in 1052. Edward was now so lacking in support that he was unable to raise an army and had to treat with Godwin: his Norman advisors were sent back to Normandy and Godwin was pardoned for his rebellion and restored to all his lands and titles. The following year Godwin died to be succeeded by his son Harold, who now became the most powerful noble in the land.

Edward never fully regained his people's faith and support but had learned to listen to the Witan, duly chastised he put all his energies into building Westminster Abbey in London; and when his army needed a leader he appointed Harold.

In January 1066 Edward the Confessor died in his early sixties on January 5, 1066, and Harold Godwinson became king. Edward was buried in Westminster Abbey and cannonized in 1161; from the mid-12th century until 1348 he was the patron saint of England.

Harold Godwinson

House of Wessex
c. 1022–1056 (r. January 5–October 14, 1066)

Although king for only ten months Harold is an important figure in English history; after him the crown passed into unpopular foreign, Norman hands, and the Anglo-Saxons became oppressed in their own land.

Harold was the second son of the powerful Earl Godwin of Wessex and his wife Gytha. While still a child, in 1044 he became the Earl of East Anglia and then as a young man in 1051 shared his father's banishment but went with his brother Leofwine to Ireland. When his father was restored to his lands and titles, Harold was similarly restored to his. When Earl Godwin died in 1053 Harold became the Earl of Wessex, making him the most powerful noble in the land; then in 1058 he also became the Earl of Hereford.

Edward the Confessor and Harold reached an accord and Harold became his principal advisor, although the pair were hardly close. In 1055 when the Welsh came and burned Hereford, Harold was at the head of the army; then, in 1063 together with his brother Tostig he campaigned in the great Welsh war and crushed Gruffydd ap Llywelyn of Gwynedd, the conqueror of Wales, who was subsequently murdered by his own followers. When Siward of Northumberland died in 1055, Tostig was given the earldom but within ten years the locals had rebelled against him and installed Morkere instead. Harold was sent as mediator and negotiated a peace which confirmed Morkere and banished Tostig.

In 1064 one of the great controversies of English history may or may not have occurred. According to Norman sources, Harold was shipwrecked off Normandy and was captured by Guy I, Duke of Ponthieu. When Duke William heard about the prisoner he demanded that he was handed over to him and then demanded that Harold swear allegiance to him personally and that he support his claim to the throne of England. Norman sources also claim that Harold was journeying to see Duke William as he had been charged by Edward the Confessor to tell him that he was his appointed heir to the throne of England. None of this is supported by Anglo-Saxon sources.

Edward appointed Harold as his successor on his deathbed and was crowned king in Westminster Abbey, but his rivals had their own ambitions. Between May and September Harold's armies fought off invasions by land and sea. From the southeast William of Normandy demanded the crown saying Edward had nominated him and that Harold himself had pledged to support him. From the north Tostig appeared and attacked the Isle of Wight but was forced to flee to Scotland. However, as fall arrived Harold ran out of money and provisions and the land army was dispersed back to their homes.

Harold moved to London and prepared to fight. His brother Tostig now allied with Harald III (Harala Hardrada) of Norway and together they sailed up the River Humber and took the city of York. Harold and his army rushed north and on

Above: A medieval representation of the death of Harold. *The Art Archive AA332588*

Left: The Bayeux Tapestry's graphic representation of the arrow hitting Harold. *via Jo St. Mart*

September 25 the two armies met at Stamford Bridge: Harold was victorious and both Tostig and Harald III were killed in battle. Duke William of Normandy seized his opportunity–and a prevailing wind–and set sail for England. He landed with his army at Pevensey. Harold, on receiving the news, gathered as many of his men as possible–bar the northerners who remained to protect their lands–and marched south to London where the call went out for men all over southern and eastern England to gather. Then, a week later, with the hastily gathered troops he marched south to Sussex where the Battle of Hastings took place. the fighting started on the morning of October 14, 1066, and lasted through the day until by evening the Normans were victorious. Harold and his brothers Leofwine and Gyrth died in the fighting. The last Anglo-Saxon king of England was dead.

Harold had married twice: initially in a Nordic marriage (ie not sanctioned by the church) to Ealdgyth Swan-neck and together they had at least four children. Then in January 1066 he married Edith, daughter of the Earl of Mercia and widow of Gruffydd ap Llywelyn of Gwynedd, whom he had defeated in 1063. She bore him twin boys, Harold and Ulf, after their father died. What became of the queen and her sons is unknown; they probably fled into exile where they lived out the remainder of their lives.

Above: There are regular reenactments of the Battle of Hastings. *Hastings Tourism via Jo St. Mart*

Edgar the Aetheling
House of Wessex
c. 1051–c. 1126

The last English heir to the English throne was born in Hungary the grandson of King Edmund II and son of Edward the Exile, and was proclaimed king but never crowned.

In 1057 when Edward the Exile died, Edgar became Edward the Confessor's heir, but when the Confessor died in 1066 Edgar was too young to take the throne at a time of such great danger to the kingdom so the Witan elected Harold Godwinson, the Confessor's brother-in-law king instead–he may well have been King Edward's choice anyway. When Harold died at the Battle of Hastings Edgar was proclaimed king by the Witan at the age of around 14, but there was no army or indeed any military support to reinforce his position. Within eight weeks he was captured and taken to Berkhamsted to submit to William the Conqueror.

King William recognized Edgar's importance and eventually shipped him to Normandy. In 1068 he escaped to Scotland where King Malcolm III gave him shelter and support. For the rest of his life he made repeated but futile attempts to regain his crown and in 1098 went to the rescue of the First Crusade by taking reinforcements to the Crusaders at the siege of Antioch.

He was eventually pardoned by King Henry I and allowed to live on his estate in Hertfordshire. It is thought he lived until his early seventies.

William I the Conqueror
House of Normandy
c. 1028–1087 (r. 1066–1087)

Guillaume le Batard or William the Bastard, was the illegitimate and only son of Duke Robert I of Normandy and Herleve, the daughter of a tanner from Falaise, where William was born. Most unusually William was recognized as his father's heir on his death in 1035– children born out of wedlock were almost always barred from inheriting. While still a child (he was eight when he inherited) his great uncle looked after the Duchy of Normandy and King Henri I of France knighted him at the age of 15.

Normandy was a powerful and rebellious duchy and a real rival for the king of France and a target for

Left: William as shown in the Bayeux Tapestry. *via Jo St. Mart*

ambitious men. The Normans were extremely warlike and raised their children in strict martial tradition so they were born to fight. William grew up to be a successful commander with a fearsome reputation who unified his lands despite many attacks on them. In 1053 he made an important dynastic marriage to his distant cousin Matilda, the daughter of Count Baldwin V of Flanders; together they had four sons and six daughters.

Normandy was not big enough for William's ambition: he wanted to be king of England, and founded his claim through being the grandnephew of Queen Emma of Normandy, the wife of both Ethelred the Unready and King Canute. He insisted that his distant cousin, Edward the Confessor, had made him his heir in 1052 and that Harold had sworn to support his claim to the throne in 1064, and that Harold was therefore a usurper. In this he was endorsed by Pope Alexander II and Emperor Henry IV.

For seven months William laid his plans and prepared his fleet; the cross-Channel invasion force consisted of around 600 ships which would carry some 3,000 cavalrymen and their horses and 4,000 infantrymen. When they were ready all they had to do was wait for a favorable wind which finally blew in on September 28.

The invasion landed unopposed at Pevensey Bay and within a few days, with ruthless Norman efficiency, they had made fortifications at Hastings in Sussex.

Left: William I grants land to Alain de Brittany. *History Department, UCL via Jo St. Mart*

Meanwhile, two days earlier, his rival Harold had won a stunning victory at Stamford Bridge against Tostig and the King of Norway in the far north of England near York. With barely time to catch his breath, Harold had to turn his army round and march back south to repel the Norman invasion. The army marched down to London where they regrouped for a week, recruited reinforcements, and within nine days were ready for battle in Sussex.

The two armies met at Senlac on October 14: Harold's veteran troops comprised the best infantry in Europe but were weary from the forced march and bulked out with inexperienced soldiers. Facing them was an equal sized army comprising Norman cavalry and archers. The battle lasted from morning till night with the Normans attacking and the English defending; no side gained an advantage. It is said that three horses were killed under Duke William during the day. In one of the final attacks Harold was killed; his two brothers also died. At dusk and without their leader the English troops panicked and fled leaving the Normans victorious. Instead of submitting to the inevitable, the Witan proclaimed Edgar Aetheling king of England leaving William no choice but to march on London. His advance was initially repelled until he met Edgar and received his submission at Berkhamsted.

On Christmas Day 1066 William I was crowned king of England at Westminster Abbey. For the next six years he battled to conquer England itself and to maintain his iron grip on Normandy. French became the language of the nobility, he introduced the Norman feudal system to England–

whereby every man in the land was pledged on pain of death to support his social superior, all the way up to the king. Uprisings were ruthlessly put down with the help of newly appointed earls who were given land in return for

Above: William the Conqueror's statue at Falaise in Normandy. He was born in Falaise Castle in 1028. *iStockphoto via Jo St. Mart*

Above: William I as depicted in an 11th century manuscript. *The Art Archive/British Library AA348739*

fighting to enforce the Norman Conquest. The English nobility had their lands and wealth confiscated and reallocated to loyal Norman nobles. The Danes were repelled and the northern nobles subjugated in Mercia and Northumbria; agricultural land was laid waste creating a famine which lasted some nine years

or so. He invaded Scotland in 1072 and established a peace, and in 1081 did much the same in Wales. The last serious English rebellion was the Revolt of the Earls in 1075.

To reinforce Norman dominance over the land William started an extensive program of castle building; over 80 had been built by the time of his death, and many of these had private armies to defend them. Additionally about half of England's landed wealth by then belonged to a favored few Normans and only two English noblemen had retained their estates.

England had become a closely administered and controlled land, but all this fighting and building cost huge amounts of money so William ordered a thorough investigation of the exact holdings of each of his feudal tenants. The resulting two-volume Domesday Book of 1086 was compiled within a remarkably short time given the complexity of its requirements. From these records William could immediately see who owned what, where, and more importantly, the fealty and tax owed to the crown.

Once England was completely subjugated William left the country to be ruled by regents while he defended Normandy against the ambitions of the French king. In fact he spent much of his last 15 years in Normandy, finally dying there on September 9, 1087, from injuries he sustained when he fell off his horse during the siege of Mantes. Before his death he divided his kingdom between his sons: Normandy went to the eldest, Robert, and England to William Rufus, his third son Henry was given 5,000 pounds in silver. William

was buried in the abbey he founded, St. Stephen at Caen.

William II Rufus
House of Normandy
c. 1056–1100 (r. 1087–1100)

Nicknamed for his ruddy appearance, William Rufus was the third and favorite son of William I and Matilda of Flanders, and was born in Normandy before his father conquered England. The Anglo-Saxon Chronicle, admittedly a very biased record, labelled him as being "hated by almost all his people." In all probability he hated his English subjects every bit as much. Very little is known about his early life, but he was almost certainly brought up in the harsh environs of the Norman court with its martial attitudes and strictures. When William I died in 1087 he bequethed the Duchy of Normandy to his eldest son, Robert Curthose, and because his second son Richard had died, England to William Rufus.

William II was crowned by Lanfranc, Archbishop of Canterbury, on September 26, 1087, and in the following year faced a short-lived rebellion led by his uncle Bishop Odo of Bayeux to force the English crown into Duke Robert's hands–but the latter was unwilling to fight in England and the English nobles instead supported William. The cause was initially supported by the Norman nobles who had lands on both sides of the Channel and supposed their fortunes would prosper under one ruler.

In 1089 William announced his intention to claim Normandy and in

Below: William II was named Rufus for his ruddy complexion.—as shown here.
History Department, UCL via Jo St. Mart

1091 invaded Normandy and forced Robert to submit to him. To occupy his time Robert went on the First Crusade in 1096 and mortgaged Normandy to William for 10,000 marks: William raised the money by imposing a heavy tax on his resentful English subjects.

When King Malcolm III of Scotland attempted to invade northern England in 1091 he was compelled to submit to William instead at the Firth of Forth. He attempted to rebel again in November 1093 but his army was beaten near Alnwick and Malcolm was killed. From then on the Scottish kings were Norman vassals.

William's relations with the church were never cordial, they disapproved of his lifestyle and court and particularly of his using church revenues for himself if he kept the bishoprics vacant. When the Archbishop of Canterbury, Anselm of Bec, fled to Rome and Pope Urban II and William seized his estates. The pope and William reached an accord which politically suited them both and William pocketed the revenues of the archbishopric of Canterbury for the remainder of his reign.

On August 2, 1100, William Rufus was hunting around Brockenhurst in the New Forest in Hampshire when he was shot by an arrow through the lung. It may have been assassination and the perpetrators may have been Walter Tirel, Lord of Poix–the two were alone at the time of William's death–acting on the orders of William's younger brother Henry Beauclerk, who quickly claimed the throne as Henry I. William II had not married or produced any known children. He was buried in Winchester Cathedral, Hampshire.

Henry I Beauclerc

House of Normandy
c. 1069–1135 (r. 1100–1135)

Above: A Victorian image of Henry I.
Wikipedia via Jo St. Mart

The fourth and youngest son of William I and Queen Matilda was born in Selby, Yorkshire and was probably destined for the church until fate intervened. Called Beauclerc for his education and learning, he was possibly the first Norman king to be fluent in English.

When his brother William II died in a hunting "accident," Henry acted quickly. His older brother Robert, Duke of Normandy, was away on the First Crusade, so Henry seized the Royal Treasury at Winchester—and buried his brother there—then had himself crowned three days later at Westminster Abbey. He bought the support of the influential barons by granting them huge favors, abolishing a number of abuses, and granting a huge range of concessions in the Charter of Liberties. Finally, to secure his northern border against invasion, he married Edith, the daughter of Malcolm III, King of Scotland: she was descended from Edward the Confessor so the marriage united the old English line of kings with the Norman newcomers, which was popular with his Anglo-Saxon subjects. But the marriage was unpopular with the Norman barons and Edith soon changed her name to Matilda to temper their feelings.

In 1101 Robert invaded England, but the brothers quickly reached a settlement in the Treaty of Alton: in return for relinquishing his claim to England Robert received Henry's Norman lands plus 2,000 silver marks annually. But Robert proved a poor leader and Henry used the excuse to invade Normandy in 1106 where he triumphed at the Battle of Tinchebrai. Robert was captured and held prisoner (in the Tower of London, Devizes Castle, and Cardiff) until his death 28 years later.

Because of his dual territories Henry was frequently absent from England so to maintain good governance in his absence—and raise crucial revenues—he created an efficient centralized bureaucracy, and also restored the laws of Edward the Confessor. The exchequer

Below: Henry I dreams about discontented peasants and angry barons. *The Art Archive/ Corpus Christi College, Oxford AA347108*

was established to look after and raise royal monies and a royal justice system put in place which toured the land to enforce local administration by investigating corruption and to raise revenues.

To keep his Norman possession Henry had to fight off the resentful barons, but their threat had disappeared by 1120. In 1113 Henry betrothed his only legitimate son, William Adelin, to the daughter of his powerful enemy, Fulk, Count of Anjou; they married in 1119. However, William was drowned in the shipwreck of the White Ship in the English Channel in 1120 throwing the succession to the crown into turmoil. Henry responded by summoning Matilda, widow of Holy Roman Emperor Henry V and his only living legitimate child, back to England. He insisted that his barons pledge their allegiance to her as his heir. To strengthen her position in 1128 she was married to her cousin Geoffrey Plantagenet, the son of Fulk V, Count of Anjou. Queen Matilda had died in 1118 and in January 1121 Henry married for a second time in an attempt to father a legitimate male successor. His wife was Adeliza, daughter of Godfrey of Leuven, but their union was childless.

Throughout his life Henry had many mistresses and up to 25 illegitimate children; many of them were ennobled, but Henry made it clear that they would never inherit his lands or crown.

Henry died from "a surfeit of lampreys" on December 1, 1135, in Saint-Denis-en-Lyons, Normandy aged about 67 while visiting his daughter Matilda, her husband, and children. His body was returned to England for burial at Reading Abbey in Berkshire.

Stephen
House of Normandy
c. 1097–1154 (r. 1135–1154)

The last Norman king of England, Stephen of Blois was born in Blois, France, the son of the Count of Blois and Adela, daughter of William the Conqueror, but he was raised at the court of his uncle Henry I in England. When Henry I died in 1135 leaving his daughter Matilda as heir, many of the barons were unhappy at having a female monarch even though they had pledged to support her. Instead the majority of the barons declared Stephen king, possibly because they knew he was a weak man who they could control, whereas Matilda was a strong woman they couldn't; Pope Innocent II also supported Stephen. Furthermore, Stephen claimed that Henry had named him successor on his deathbed.

Above: Stephen was crowned at Winchester on December 26, 1135, and again at Canterbury on December 25, 1141.
History Department, UCL via Jo St. Mart

In 1139 England was plunged into the "Anarchy"–a period of civil war that started when Matilda's half-brother Robert, Earl of Gloucester, fought on her behalf. Initially Stephen's armies won many of the battles, but in September 1139 Matilda invaded England and took control of western England. Two years later, in spring 1141, Stephen was defeated and captured in battle at Lincoln. He was imprisoned in Bristol until November that year when he was exchanged for the captured Earl of Gloucester. In his absence Stephen's wife–also called Matilda–had rallied support from the barons and from Londoners. Gradually Stephen's forces prevailed until in 1148 Matilda left England altogether.

In such times of unrest the barons consolidated personal control of their territories and areas of influence, and Stephen had little power over his land or nobles. He intended to leave the throne to his son Eustace, but he died in 1153 and although he still had a living son in William of Blois, Stephen reluctantly agreed to hand the succession to Matilda's son Henry, as stipulated in the Treaty of Wallingford.

Stephen died in October 1154 at Dover Priory in Kent and was buried at Faversham Abbey. He joined his wife, Matilda, daughter of the Count of Boulogne, whom he had married around 1125. She had died in 1152 and was buried in the abbey she and her husband had founded.

Henry II Curtmantle
House of Plantagenet
1133–1189 (r. 1154–1189)

Henry was the first Plantagenet king and one of the most successful and powerful kings in English history: as the beneficiary of three enormous dynasties he ruled lands from the Solway Firth in the north to the Pyrenees in the south. He was the son of Geoffrey Plantagenet (Geoffrey V of Anjou) and Matilda of England, and was born in Le Mans, northwest France. Brought up in Anjou, at age nine he was taken to Bristol in England to continue his education.

When only 19 years old in 1152 Henry quietly married Eleanor of Aquitaine in Bordeaux Cathedral on May 18, 1152. The reason for discretion was that only six weeks previously Eleanor had had her marriage to King Louis VII of France annulled on the grounds of consanguinity (they were already estranged and Louis was desperate for a male heir). Although about 11 years older, Eleanor was a prize catch as since the age of 15 she had become the wealthiest woman in Europe–the heiress to Aquitaine, the largest and richest province of France. Over the years of their tempestuous

Left: Henry II leads his wife, Eleanor of Aquitaine, and son Richard into captivity after the 1173 revolt—from a fresco, Chapelle de Sainte Radegonde, Chinon. *The Art Archive/ Gianni Dagli Orti AA371487*

Right: Statue of Henry II. *Lichfield Cathedral via Jo St. Mart*

marriage (which was even more consanguinious than her previous marriage) they had five sons and three daughters–William (died aged two and a half), Henry (the "Young King," died of dysentry in 1183), Richard (King Richard the Lionheart), Geoffrey (died age 28 in Paris), John (King John I), Matilda (married Henry the Lion, Duke of Saxony and Bavaria), Eleanor (married Alfonso VIII of Castile), and Joan (married William II of Sicily). In addition Henry complicated matters further by also fathering a number of illegitimate children.

From his father Henry inherited Maine and Anjou while from his mother he received Normandy. When he married Eleanor of Aquitaine he added control (though not ownership which remained hers) of Aquitaine and Gascony–all of which made him Louis VII's most powerful (and feared) vassal. Also through his mother, Empress Matilda, he had a strong claim to the throne of England.

Henry journeyed to England at the head of an army three times–in 1147, 1149, and 1150–without success, until in January 1153 he arrived on the south coast with 36 ships and 3,000 soldiers. With much popular support he managed to secure King Stephen's agreement to make him his heir with the Treaty of Wallingford (1153). Stephen died in October 1154 and Henry became king at the age of 22 already well versed in the deadly games of intrigue and diplomacy. He was crowned at Westminster Abbey on December 19, 1154.

As king his first job was to reunite the kingdom so ineptly ruled by Stephen and still suffering from the divisiveness of the civil war. He started tearing down the rebel castles which had been built by rogue barons during Stephen's reign and imposed a new tax known as "scutage" by which means the barons–who had got used to avoiding military service–paid instead for the king to hire mercenaries to do the fighting for them without any of the danger of the barons becoming too powerful and turning on the king.

Above: Henry II performing his penance before the shrine of Thomas Becket. *The Art Archive/Bibliothèque des Arts Décoratifs Paris/Gianni Dagli Orti AA41990I*

Realizing that the key to good governance was real justice and fair laws, Henry set about reforming English law (with the help of his chancellor Thomas Becket) and consequently has been credited as the founder of English Common Law. In the Assize of Clarendon in 1166 he established a new procedure for criminal justice, establishing Royal Magistrate courts which gave appointed court officials the power to adjudicate in the name of the crown on local matters, new prisons for people awaiting trial, and the first juries started to pronounce on legal matters. Local sheriffs became appointed agents with powers to enforce the law and collect taxes across the land. By 1158 Henry had restored much of the royal power and retrieved once lost lands.

Physically imposing, Henry loved the rigors of hunting–but he was as well a man of letters and scholarly debate. He was also feared for his volcanic and sudden temper. He would sit in on his councils whenever possible and enjoyed the intricacies of the law.

The church was a thorn in Henry's side so he sought to limit its control and in particular reduce interference from the pope and his advisors. Henry increasingly authorized the use of secular courts for dealing with ecclesiastical disputes, but, the new Archbishop of Canterbury, his one-time chancellor and great friend, Thomas Becket, refused to ratify Henry's proposals and attempted to block any increase of royal power over church affairs. Becket fled to France and the protection of Louis VII when Henry ordered him to appear before the Royal Council to explain himself, and only returned in 1170 when Henry promised that he wouldn't punish him. But Henry was still infuriated by Becket's intransigence and—it has gone done in history—shouted out in anger, "Who will rid me of this turbulent priest?" Possibly misinterpreting Henry's intentions, four of his knights—Hugh de Moreville, Richard le Breton, William de Tracy, and Reginald Fitzurse—rode out for Canterbury on December 29, 1170. They found Becket in the cathedral and beat him to death on holy ground.

Henry was hugely remorseful and denied any intention for harm to come to his former friend. In 1172 Henry was compelled by the popular backlash against the murder to sign the Compromise of Avranches which relinquished all secular jurdisdiction over the clergy. Within three years Pope Alexander III declared Becket a saint and martyr for the church.

An Irish dissident and minor prince, Diarmait Mac Murchada was driven off his lands in Leinster and appealed to Henry II for help. This invitation suited

Above: Beckett arguing with Henry II from a manuscript by Peter Langtoft, 1300. *The Art Archive/British Library AA348521*

Henry's political ambitions and after restoring Diarmait to his lands, in 1171 Henry declared himself Lord of Ireland, a title he later gave to his son John: so starting 800 years of English domination of Ireland. A few years later in 1174 King William the Lion of Scotland invaded northern England at the same time as a Flemish armada was threatening the south. Henry, seeing the hand of an angry God in the threats, hastily made for Canterbury where he did penance for the murder of Archbishop Thomas Becket. The armada dispersed without landing and Henry sent his army north to face the Scottish invaders. The armies met at the Battle of Alnwick: King William was captured and the Scots routed leaving Henry with control over southern Scotland.

Now Henry's greatest troubles came from his immediate family, all of whom quarreled incessantly and violently. Dubbed "the Angevin Curse" his

problem was how to divide his lands and wealth among his children in such a way that each would be satisfied with their portion and not wage war on each other. His second son, Richard, refused to submit to Henry's nominated successor, Young Henry, his older brother, and both wanted their inheritance immediately. They rebelled (encouraged by Queen Eleanor) but were quickly crushed by their father. Eleanor was punished by being placed under house arrest for the next 16 years of her life.

In 1182, Young Henry, Richard, and Geoffrey—each encouraged by King Philip Augustus of France—began fighting each other for their father's French territories. But in June the following year Young Henry suddenly died and the threat dissipated until 1184 when Geoffrey and John invaded Aquitaine only to be defeated by their brother Richard. In the next couple of years Geoffrey died and John clearly became his father's favorite and possible nominated successor: fearing the loss of his due inheritance as oldest son, Richard allied with Philip Augustus and together in summer 1189 successfully invaded Anjou. In defeat Henry II was forced to agree to all their demands, notably reinstating Richard as heir and paying homage to Philip Augustus for his French possessions.

Henry was by now 56 years old, ill, and deserted by almost all his family: he died at Chinon castle on July 6, 1189, from where he was taken to be buried at nearby Fontevraud Abbey. In total Henry had spent 21 years of his reign in his French territories and only 13 years in England.

Richard I Lionheart (Coeur de Lion)

House of Plantagenet
1157–1199 (r. 1189–1199)

Called Coeur de Lion for his bravery and fighting spirit—he was already commanding his father's army at the age of 16—Richard I proved an expensive monarch. Before becoming king he repeatedly campaigned against both his father and his brothers for lands, wealth, and influence—particularly in France—and although burningly ambitious to be rich and powerful, after becoming king, Richard was happy to leave his lands under the control of others while he went to fight in foreign lands.

Born into a notoriously quarrelsome and jealous family at Beaumont Palace in Oxford, Richard was the second son of King Henry II and Eleanor of Aquitaine. When his parents separated he stayed with Eleanor who gave him her duchy in 1168, then Poitiers in 1172.

In spring 1174 Richard joined causes with his brothers John and Geoffrey and rebelled against his father; in the end they all capitulated with Richard refusing to fight his own father in single combat. In 1179 Richard scored a remarkable victory at the seemingly impregnable fortress of Taillebourg, this sealed his reputation as a clever and ruthless commander and deterred many other would-be insurgents from rebelling. While campaigning in France he assembled a reputation for cruelty and ruthlessness.

Left: The spoils of war—Richard I on crusade. *The Art Archive/National Museum Damascus Syria/Gianni Dagli Orti AA386672*

Above: This statue of Richard I by Carlo Marochetti stands near the Houses of Parliament in London. *Jo St. Mart*

In 1183 when Young Henry died, Richard became heir to the throne of England, but his father wanted John to have Aquitaine. Richard was furious and in 1189 allied with his friend Philip II Augustus of France against his father. The pair triumphed and Richard was again restored to his full inheritance.

When Henry II died in 1189 Richard became king of England, Duke of Normandy, and Count of Anjou and was crowned at Westminster Abbey on September 13, 1189. But Richard longed to go on crusade and fight for the return of the Holy Land–in 1187 Saladin had captured the Holy City of Jerusalem. When the Third Crusade was raised to counter his victory Richard was determined to join. Across the Channel King Philip also agreed to go.

To pay for the crusade Richard spent most of the money in the treasury, then raised taxes and sold various local offices, official positions, lands, and rights until he had sufficient funds to leave England in 1190. He is reported to have said, "I would have sold London if I could find a buyer." The governance of England was left largely in the hands of his mother, Eleanor of Aquitaine, and his French lands in various hands, most notably William Fitz Ralph who was appointed seneschal of Normandy.

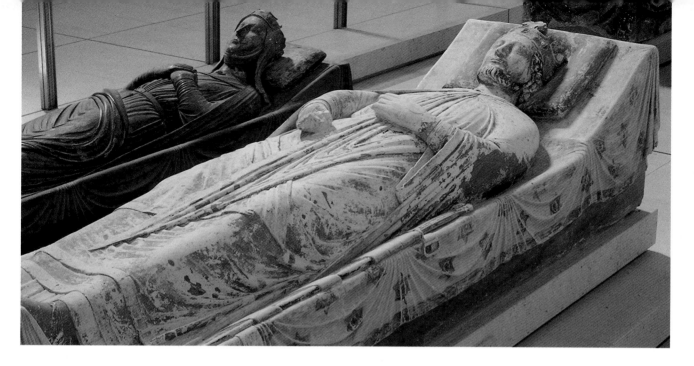

Above: Richard I was buried at Fontevraud Abbey near Chinon in Anjou—once the resting place of many of his family. Today only the effigies of Henry II, Eleanor, and—as seen here—Richard, and Isabella (wife of Richard's younger brother John) can be seen. *Wikipedia via Jo St. Mart*

Left: A bowman readies to fire the arrow that would ultimately kill Richard I at Châlus. *The Art Archive AA348085*

Richard left England with a fleet of 100 ships carrying 4,000 men at arms and 4,000 foot soldiers. On the way they occupied and pacified Sicily, and by May they had arrived in Cyprus, which Richard conquered. He then married Berengaria, the daughter of King Sancho VI of Navarre, and by June 1191 he arrived in the Holy Land. In July he captured the great castle at Acre, and in September Richard succeeded at Arsuf and the Crusaders were able to take Jaffa (1192), but he never set foot in Jerusalem. Aside fighting the infidel, the various national contingencies–French, German, and English–continuously fell out with each other. A year's stalemate followed, after which Richard reached a truce with Saladin and packed up to return home.

Meanwhile, back in western Europe Philip II Augustus attempted unsuccessfully to take possession of Richard's French territories, and in England his brother John occupied Windsor Castle and prepared an invasion force of Flemish mercenaries. However, Queen Eleanor responded by prising oaths of allegiance from the barons and strengthening the garrisons across the country. It is during this period that the stories of Robin Hood are set.

Richard's journey home was not easy: a storm drove his ship ashore near Aquileia in the Adriatic near Venice and he was imprisoned by Leopold of Austria, who soon handed him over to Henry VI, the Holy Roman Emperor, in 1193. Henry ransomed Richard for the enormous sum of 150,000 silver marks. The money was raised and in February 1194 Richard was released and rushed to England where he was crowned for a second time at Winchester to reinforce his authority and assure his people of his independence from foreign influence. Within a month he journeyed to Normandy to inspect his French territories and never again returned to England.

Richard I spent his next five years intermittently fighting against Philip II Augustus. His final battle was the siege of Châlus in central France where he received a fatal wound and died on April 6, 1199. Richard was King of England for ten years, he barely spoke English and spent a total of only six months in England while king.

John I Lackland

House of Plantagenet
1167–1216 (r. 1199–1216)

Son of King Henry II and Eleanor of Aquitaine, and younger brother of Richard Coeur de Lion, John was born at Beaumont Palace, Oxford, rebelled against his father (although he was his favorite son) and fought with and against his brothers for lands and titles. He had received a thorough and excellent education but even so, when in 1185 he was made the ruler of Ireland, his ruthlessness and cruelty made him hugely unpopular and he had to leave after only eight months.

In October 1190 Richard named his nephew Arthur (their brother Geoffrey's son), as his heir instead of John, so infuriating the latter that when Richard was away on the Third Crusade John attempted a royal coup. His mother Eleanor defended her absent son's possessions, but the brothers were reconciled on Richard's return and when Arthur was captured by Philip II Augustus in 1196, Richard named John as his heir.

In 1189 John married Isabel of Gloucester but they had no children and John successfully applied for an annulment on the grounds of consanguinity around the time he became king of England (1199). The next year in August, John kidnapped and married his second wife, Isabella of Angoulême, from her betrothed Hugh de Lusignan. Together they had two sons and three daughters, although John had numerous illegitimate children as well.

Deeply insulted the Lusignans rebelled and appealed to Philip II Augustus for help. He ordered John to appear before him to explain, but John never appeared: instead war was declared. By 1206 John had lost Normandy, and his mother's inheritance lands of Anjou, Maine, and parts of Poitou (Eleanor had died in 1204). In order to win back the lost territories John raised punitive taxes from England and demanded in full all his feudal rights, making him ever more unpopular.

John quarreled badly with the church over the appointment of the Archbishop of Canterbury which led Pope Innocent III in 1207 to impose an interdict on England—meaning no church services or rituals, such as the last rites–in the hope and expectation that the people of England

Above: Victorian impression of John. *The Art Archive AA374639*

Above right: Beautiful 14th century manuscript illustration showing King John stag hunting. *The Art Archive/British Library/Harper Collins Publishers AA347284*

Right: John's tomb is in Worcester cathedral. The Purbeck marble sarcophagus lid effigy dates from about 1240 and is believed to be the earliest portrait of an English king; the rest of the tomb dates from 1540. *History Department, UCL via Jo St. Mart*

On June 15, the two sides met at Runnymede on Charter Island in the River Thames and there King John agreed to limits on his power as king and pledged to respect feudal rights and English law in a document called Magna Carta, signed on June 18, 1215.

The two sides soon fell out again and the barons invited Prince Louis of France to England to become king. John's armies laid waste to the north of England and areas around the border with Scotland. While returning south John took a route around the marshy Wash to avoid rebel-held East Anglia, but sent his slow baggage train which was carrying the crown jewels directly across the sands. The incoming tide swept away the baggage train causing John considerable anguish. His health and state of mind suffered and he soon fell sick to a bout of dysentery: he died at Newark Castle on October 18 and was buried at Worcester Cathedral.

Without the main protagonist in the civil war a compromise peace was soon reached, which restored their rights to the barons who switched their allegiance to John's nine-year-old son, Henry instead of the foreigner Louis.

would rise up against their king. John seized all church property in response and even after three years of interdiction the people did not rebel. So, in November 1209 John was excommunicated and England threatened with a crusade led by Philip II Augustus who would put his son Louis on the throne. Knowing his rebellious barons would likely support the crusade, John submitted to the Pope, made England a papal fief, and won the pope's support against the barons.

Civil war broke out in May 1215. The rebels seized London and John was forced to negotiate from a position of weakness.

Henry III

House of Plantagenet
1207–1272 (r. 1216–1272)

Henry III's reign is characterized by continuous strife and civil war with the barons and repeated failure to recapture lost French lands. Born in Winchester Castle the son of King John and Isabella of Angoulême, Henry was only nine years old when he became king of England and hastily crowned in Gloucester Cathedral. His French rival Louis was also proclaimed king by a majority of disgruntled barons, but the rebels quickly realized that Henry–advised and guided by his regents–William Marshall, 1st Earl of Pembroke (died May 1219) and Hubert de Burgh, 1st Earl of Kent–would be a better option. The French were quicky thrown out of London and the Channel ports and order was restored in England.

Throughout his teenage years Henry was anxious to become king in his own right and reestablish the Anglo-Norman autocratic monarchy–something his barons were equally anxious to avoid. Aged 19, in 1227 Henry reached his majority and assumed power, but kept de Burgh as his chief advisor. In January 1236 Henry married the beautiful Eleanor of Provence and together they had five children.

Above: Although generally unpopular, Henry III ruled for 56 years. *History Department, UCL via Jo St. Mart*

Left: Henry III during his coronation, he is holding a model of Westminster Abbey. *History Department, UCL via Jo St. Mart*

One of Henry's greatest mistakes that was instrumental in alienating the barons even further was appointing his and his wife's French relatives to positions of power and importance. Added to this his repeated expensive and futile attempts to regain the lost lands proved disastrous.

The English barons were deeply unhappy about foreign influence in the country and rallied round Simon de Montfort in rebellion. In essence they wanted a return to the laws of Magna Carta and more powers for themselves. Finally, in 1258 Henry was forced by seven barons to sign and swear an oath to uphold the Provisions of Oxford which abolished the absolutist Anglo-Norman monarchy and established a privy council of 15 barons to advise the king and oversee the legislature and administration, and the gathering of a parliament three times a year.

The following year the Provisions of Westminster also attempted to control the king and establish common law. Within two years the king broke his word (with a papal bull exempting him) and the second barons' war broke out. Following the Battle of Lewes in May 1264, Henry and his son Edward (later Edward I) were captured and placed under house arrest and de Montfort assumed government.

After 15 months Edward escaped his captors while hunting and led his supporters to victory against Simon de Montford at the Battle of Evesham (1265). De Montfort was killed and a new government set up; in 1267 in the Statute of Marlborough Henry promised to uphold Magna Carta and some of the Provisions of Westminster.

Above left: Gold coin showing Henry III holding the orb and scepter. *The Art Archive/ British Museum/Eileen Tweedy AA347104*

Above: Henry II (above left), Richard I (above right), John (below left), and Henry III (below right), from Matthew Paris's *Historia Anglorum*, 1250. *The Art Archive/British Library AA347220*

Henry died in 1272 aged 65 after reigning for 56 years. He was eventually buried in Westminster Abbey. Under his aegis Westminster had become the primary seat of power in England.

Edward I Longshanks
House of Plantagenet
1239–1307 (r. 1272–1307)

Born in Westminster Palace, Edward was the son of Henry III and Eleanor of Provence who made sure he had a thorough and disciplined education. He almost died aged seven but was nursed through illness by his mother at Beaulieu Abbey.

When aged 15 in November 1254 Edward journeyed to Spain where he married his second cousin–they were both descendants of Henry II–Leonora (Eleanor) of Castile (daughter of the King of Castile and only 13). It proved a love match and they had 16 children together. To provide him with an income his father gave him the duchy of Gascony, which included the Channel Islands, lands in Wales, and parts of Ireland.

In August 1270 Edward–with wife Eleanor and brother Edmund–joined King Louis IX and the Eighth Crusade to raise the siege of Acre and relieve the Christian garrison and recover the Holy Land. To fund the trip a levy of one-twentieth of every citizen's goods and possessions was imposed. The party spent the winter in Sicily and arrived in Palestine in May 1271. Louis IX died of plague in Tunis, but Edward decided to continue the crusade. While in the Holy Land in June 1272, he narrowly escaped an assassination attempt by a member of the Assassins equipped with a poisoned dagger employed by one of the Emirs. He managed a miraculous recovery and a ten-year truce between

Above: Edward I from a stained glass window. *The Art Archive/Bibliothèque des Arts Décoratifs Paris/Gianni Dagli Orti AA419902*

the Moslems and Christians of Acre was negotiated, despite Edward's objections. Edward was still in the Holy Land when his father died leaving him unopposed king of England in November 1272; however, he did not reach London until August 1274 when he was crowned at Westminster Abbey aged 35.

Initially calling himself Edward IV he quickly changed this to become Edward I. At his first parliament, in the Statute of Westminster, he legislated on

the laws of England to refine and bring them up to date. Then in 1274 he ordered a country-wide survey into the usurpation of crown lands and rights which had been lost during the upheavaals of his father's reign.

Edward was an ambitious king and once he had England under control he resolved to conquer the numerous princedoms of Wales. In 1277 he led his army into North Wales where he forced the surrender of Llywellyn ap Gruffyd, Prince of Gwynedd, at the Treaty of Aberconwy in 1277. The same year Dafydd ap Gruffyd (Llywellyn's brother) led a rebellion against the English and was initially successful. Llywellyn was killed at the Battle of Irfon Bridge (1282) but Dafydd fought on until his capture and execution in 1283. To prevent further Welsh insurrection Edward embarked on a massive castle-building program–each a day's march apart.

In 1290 Queen Eleanor caught a fever and died in Nottinghamshire: Edward was devastated at her loss and ordered a memorial cross to be erected at every spot her body rested on its journey back to London, three still survive at Geddington, Northampton, and Waltham, and in name only at Charing Cross in London.

At the age of 60 Edward remarried in September 1299, choosing the 17-year-old Margaret of France, daughter of Philip III of France; together they had three children.

In Scotland, King Alexander III died leaving his granddaughter Margaret as sole heir, but she died in Orkney on her way to England where she was due to marry Edward, Prince of Wales. The Scottish lords then asked Edward to

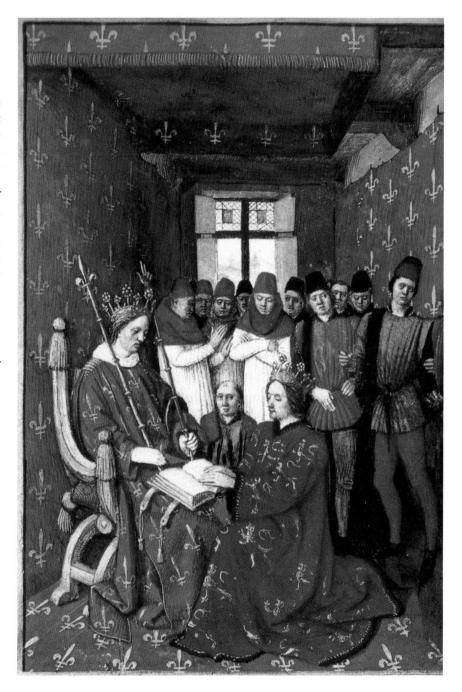

Right: Edward I in his role as Duke of Aquitaine paying homage to Philippe IV of France. *via Jo St Mart*

arbitrate between the rival candidates. Edward took full advantage of the situation to ensure that the Scottish king paid fealty to the English crown. He chose John de Balliol, who became an English puppet, and the Scottish lords rose in revolt. Edward sent his army to Scotland in 1296; the border town of Berwick-upon-Tweed was stormed and then the army moved north into Scotland. King John was captured and sent to the Tower of London. At the same time, the Stone of Scone–the ancient coronation stone of Scotland– was taken to Westminster Abbey (it was returned some 700 years later in 1996).

The new Scottish opponent was William Wallace who fought in the name of King John with the support of the clans but not the Scottish nobles; he scored a notable victory at Stirling Bridge (1297) but was defeated by Edward I at Falkirk (1298) although he escaped to fight again. Three regents were appointed to rule Scotland: the Bishop of St. Andrews, John Comyn, and Robert the Bruce. Wallace appeared again at Stirling Castle in 1304 but was taken by his own countrymen and handed over to the English who hung, drew, and quartered him. Robert the Bruce murdered his rival John Comyn and was crowned King of the Scots and attempted to turn the tide against the English invaders. Edward again returned to Scotland at the head of his army but he died at Burgh on Sands in July 1307 at the age of 68. He was buried at Westminster Abbey.

Left: Edward I and Eleanor of Castile presenting their infant son, the future Edward II, to the Welsh in 1284, from Cassell's *Illustrated History of England. The Art Archive AA526247*

Above: Bishops and monks in audience with Edward I, c. 1300. *The Art Archive/British Library AA346923*

Edward II
House of Plantagenet
1284–1327 (r. 1307–1327)

The reign of Edward II saw a constant wrestling for control of England between the king and his favorites on one side and the powerful barons on the other. Disliked by his queen and his people, Edward's openly homosexual friendships would not have brought him down had he not lavished them with titles, lands, and authority.

Edward was born the fourth son of Edward I and Eleanor of Castile at Caernarfon Castle in Wales. He was the first Englishman to become Prince of Wales. Although well educated in statecraft and military matters as befitted a future king, he had no interest in them, preferring more workmanlike pursuits. His overbearing father also detested his close friend, the Gascon knight Piers Gaveston, and exiled him to France.

When his father died, one of Edward's first moves was to recall Piers Gaveston from exile; he also abandoned the campaigns against the Scots. He allied himself dynastically to King Philip IV of France by marrying his daughter Isabella (her three brothers each in turn became kings of France) in Boulogne in January 1308. Although their marriage was far from close they had two sons, Edward and John, and two daughters, Eleanor and Joanna.

While he was in France Edward left Gaveston as regent and scandalously conferred on him the royal title of Earl of Cornwall and his niece Margaret of Gloucester in marriage. This hugely

EDWARD II.

unpopular move undermined Edward's popularity with his subjects and in 1311 his outraged nobles issued the "Ordinances" which attempted to limit the king's finances, control royal appointments, and banish Gaveston. The latter was exiled, but he returned quickly.

In 1312 the Earl of Lancaster and his allies seized and beheaded Gaveston in Warwickshire, but without the king's favorite as a focus the barons quickly fell out and a furious Edward was able to force the earls of Lancaster, Hereford, Arundel, and Warwick to beg his pardon.

The Scottish king Robert the Bruce was making trouble in the north so Edward sent an invading army to Scotland but was decisively beaten at the Battle of Bannockburn in 1314. A humbled Edward lost his power and authority to the barons who looked to Thomas of Lancaster (Edward's cousin) for leadership: he was effectively king of England by 1315. Under his custody much of the country returned to local anarchy.

Above left: Medieval statues of Edwards I, II, and III, from near the choir in York cathedral. *The Art Archive/Gianni Dagli Orti AA383835*

Above: Edward II was the first monarch to found colleges at Oxford and Cambridge universities. *via Jo St Mart*

Above right: Edward II was probably murdered by his enemies, but he was still buried in a magnificent tomb in Gloucester Cathedral. *via Jo St Mart*

By 1318 Edward and Thomas had reached a working rapprochment until Edward promoted his two new favorites, Hugh le Despenser and his son. Their greed and corruption disgusted all and they were forced into exile as civil war broke out: Edward defeated Lancaster in battle at Boroughbridge in March 1322 and executed him. The Despensers were recalled and Edward then shared his royal authority with them.

Largely ignored by her husband, Isabella of France was supported by the barons. In 1325 she was sent on a diplomatic mission to France and while there met and became the mistress of Roger Mortimer, another of Edward's exiled barons. Together they assembled an army of 1,500 mercenaries and invaded England in September 1326 to general acclaim. The Despensers were captured and executed and Edward was forced to renounce his throne in favor of his and Isabella's son, Edward. The former king was imprisoned in Berkeley Castle and was probably murdered there.

Edward III
House of Plantagenet
1312–1377 (r. 1327–1377)

A great soldier and leader, Edward III's reign saw the start of the interminable series of conflicts and wars between England and France which became known as the Hundred Years' War. Initially acclaimed, the foreign campaigning which necessitated high

taxes made Edward increasingly unpopular over the latter part of his fifty-year reign. Additionally, the Black Death—seen as God's curse—struck three times, in 1348–49, 1361–62, and 1369.

Probably born at Windsor Castle, very little is known about the early years of Edward III other than that his parents were Edward II and Isabella of France.

Edward became king at the age of 14 in 1327 when his mother and her lover, the arrogant and greedy Roger Mortimer, Earl of March, forced Edward II to renounce the throne in his favor. The pair then ruled as joint regents until 1330 when Edward, aged 17, staged a coup and took over: he exiled his mother to Castle Rising in Norfolk and executed Mortimer for usurping the throne.

In 1328, while still a minor, Edward married Phillippa of Hainault and together they had 13 children; he had no known illegitimate children. In 1337 he created the Duchy of Cornwall to provide an independent income for his oldest son, a tradition which continues to this day.

With the kingdom largely peaceful, Scotland largely quelled (by 1337), and the barons under control, Edward's primary concerns were the former French territories which had once belonged to the English crown—in 1337 Philip VI had confiscated Aquitaine and Ponthieu. Two years later Edward and his army invaded France and the following year he provocatively assumed the title King of France and so started what came to be known as the Hundred Years' War between France and England. In July 1346 Edward invaded Normandy accompanied by his son Edward, the Black Prince and 15,000 men. By August

Above: Edward III taking the city of Caen, France, in 1346, from *Froissart's Chronicles*. *The Art Archive/Bibliothèque Nationale Paris/ Harper Collins Publishers AA333932*

Left: Edward III. *The Art Archive/Bibliothèque des Arts Décoratifs Paris/Gianni Dagli Orti AA423103*

they had triumphed at the Battle of Crécy and then went on to capture the vital Channel port of Calais, which they used as their military base for French campaigns.

The war restarted in 1355 and in the following year the Black Prince not only won a magnificent victory at Poitiers but

also captured King John II of France. A peace was negotiated in which Edward renounced his claim to the French crown (in return for Aquitaine) and signed to that effect in the Treaty of Brétigny (1360) giving Edward control of almost a quarter of France: this ended the first phase of the Hundred Years'

War. But in 1369 the French declared war again. Edward was by then too old to lead his armies which he left to his sons. They soon lost almost all the territorial gains of 1360, only holding on to Calais and a piece of coast near Bordeaux, and Bayonne.

At home in England the military losses, the expense of the campaigns and crippling taxation, and the outbreak of plague led to a crisis which was furthered when the death of Queen Phillippa in 1369 saw the old king falling under the malign influence of his mistress Alice Perrers. From about this time onward Edward fell increasing ill and played little active part in ruling the country. In 1376 the "Good Parliament" was called to rectify the situation. The corruption of the court was criticized and the heavy taxes condemned; Alice Perrers was banished from court. But to make matters worse, the death of the Black Prince, heir to the throne, was announced. This left John of Gaunt, Edward's younger son and regent in his absence, as the next king.

Edward died aged 64 at Sheen Palace, Surrey in June 1377 naming his grandson Richard as king.

Richard II
House of Plantagenet
1367–1400 (r. 1377–1399)

Richard's reign saw a 28-year truce in the Hundred Years' War–although there were constant threats of a French invasion. At home although Richard started as a popular monarch, his closest friends and chosen advisors, his extravagant court, and his absolutist attitude made him unpopular with the public at large and the nobility in particular.

The grandson of Edward III and second son of Edward, the Black Prince and Joan, Countess of Kent (the Fair Maid of Kent), Richard was born in Bordeaux and became king in 1377 at the age of ten (his older brother Edward had died in 1371). During his minority and to avoid the distinct possibility of his uncle John of Gaunt, Edward III's third surviving son, usurping the crown, England was ruled through a series of "continual councils" from which Gaunt was excluded but able to exert influence.

Following the terrible toll of the Black Death in 1381 and three poll taxes levied to pay for the military campaigns in France, the peasantry of England had had enough. The Peasants' Revolt was led by Wat Tyler and demanded the abolition of serfdom. The kingdom was briefly threatened until the young king rode out to Smithfield to meet the rebels,

Left: Richard II being led by Henry Bolingbroke to London, from *l listoire du Roy d'Angleterre Richard II* by Jean Creton. *The Art Archive/British Library AA348083*

Above: Richard II and St. John the Baptist, Winchester College chapel. *Historical Department UCL/Jo St Mart*

compromise could not be reached but Tyler was taken and killed and the revolt collapsed over the next few weeks as Richard granted clemency to the rebels; once the danger of rebellion had disappeared he revoked the freedoms and pardons.

In January 1382 Richard made a politically expedient marriage to Anne of Bohemia, daughter of Holy Roman Emperor Charles IV. The union was not popular in England, Anne brought no dowry, rather Richard had to give 20,000 florins to her brother. Anne died of plague, childless in 1394.

In family tradition Richard wanted to fight in France to regain the lost lands but parliament refused to cooperate unless he got rid of his unpopular advisors—

principally Michael de la Pole, Earl of Suffolk, and Robert de Vere, Earl of Oxford. Richard refused. In response parliament impeached the Earl of Suffolk and established a commission to oversee and regulate the king's decisions and activities. Government was taken over by the Lords Appellant; a move Richard declared to be treasonous. In 1388 the "Merciless Parliament" outlawed Richard's closest friends and executed a number leaving Richard no option but to submit to the demands of the five Lords Appellant. But by May 1389 Richard was back in command of his government, promising to reduce taxation and seek peace with France. For eight years the reconciliation held. As part of the peace Richard married Isabella of Valois, the daughter of Charles VI of France.

By 1397 Richard had sufficient support to move against his enemies. He arrested and tried three of the appellants: Arundel was convicted of treason and executed; Gloucester was imprisoned and subsequently murdered; and Warwick banished. Parliament was reduced to an advisory role as Richard pocketed all the revenues of state.

Richard further strengthened his position the following fall when Henry Bolingbroke, Earl of Derby and Thomas de Mowbray quarreled and Richard banished them both. In February 1399 John of Gaunt died and Richard confiscated his vast Duchy of Lancaster estates so they could not pass to his heir Bolingbroke. Instead, he gave them to his favorites. Then, in May Richard left to campaign in Ireland.

With Richard and his army absent, Bolingbroke seized his opportunity and

invaded northern England in June 1399 to reclaim his inheritance and quickly gathered support. Richard returned to England in August and surrendered without a fight. He abdicated in September and Bolingbroke took the crown as Henry IV. In October Richard was imprisoned in Pontefract Castle but when popular risings in support of him threatened the peace he died aged 33 in mysterious circumstances—probably murdered—in February 1400. He was buried in Westminster Abbey.

Below: Richard II. *The Art Archive/Bibliothèque des Arts Décoratifs Paris/Gianni Dagli Orti AA419903*

Above: Henry IV's tomb in Canterbury cathedral. *via Jo St Mart*

Below: A gold noble of Henry IV. *The Art Archive/British Museum/Eileen Tweedy AA347105*

Henry IV Bolingbroke
House of Lancaster
1367–1413 (r. 1399–1413)

Henry Bolingbroke did not have the best claim to the throne of England, Richard II was his first cousin. Once in power Henry's greatest problems concerned Scottish border raids and renewed Hundred Years' War conflicts with France.

Born in Bolingbroke Castle in Lincolnshire in 1367 Henry was the son of John of Gaunt and Blanche of Lancaster, the pair were cousins and needed papal dispensation to marry. In July 1380 Henry married Mary de Bohun and together they had seven

children. She died in childbirth in 1394 and Henry married again in 1403 to Joanna of Navarre, daughter of Charles d'Evreux, the King of Navarre: they had no children.

In 1386 Henry Bolingbroke joined forces with an influential opposition of nobles hostile to the rule of Richard II. After numerous power struggles and quarrels, in 1398 Bolingbroke was banished from the kingdom for ten years. The following year when his father John of Gaunt died, Henry was disinherited by

Below: Detail from Henry IV's tomb. *Jo St. Mart*

his cousin Richard II and banished for life. While abroad Henry allied with the exiled Thomas Arundel, former Archbishop of Canterbury, and together they returned to England at the head of an army in 1399 and quickly acquired popular support from both nobility and peasantry alienated by Richard II. The latter, finding he had little or no popular support, surrendered to Bolingbroke and seems to have abdicated willingly. Edmund de Mortimer, 5th Earl of March,

Above: Henry, Duke of Lancaster is proclaimed King Henry IV by parliament in 1399. *The Art Archive/British Library/AA347188*

Right: The Battle of Agincourt. *History Department, UCL via Jo St. Mart*

the seven-year-old heir presumptive was imprisoned but treated well even though he was the Yorkist Pretender.

Henry Bolingbroke was crowned Henry IV in October 1399 but while establishing his superior claim to the throne he had to put down a series of small rebellions. An outbreak of Black Death in 1400 was accompanied by a rebellion in Wales led by Owen Glyndwr; three years later he then allied with the Henry Percy, Earl of Northumberland and his son Henry (Harry) Hotspur. The latter however was killed at the Battle of Shrewsbury in July 1403 and further rebels were executed in York bringing the revolt to an end.

To finance his Scottish and French adventures Henry had to petition parliament for grants of money–they were not sympathetic and instead accused him of being reckless with money, but bargained new powers over royal appointments and finances in exchange for the funds Henry needed.

From 1405 onwards Henry suffered from a debilitating skin disease, possibly leprosy, and another acute unknown illness. This left a vacancy at the head of government which his oldest son Henry was only too happy to fill. Henry died in 1413; it had been prophesied that he would died in Jerusalem: he did, the room he was taken to was the Jerusalem chamber in the house of the Abbot of Westminster. He was buried in Canterbury Cathedral near the shrine of Thomas Becket.

Henry V

House of Lancaster
1387–1422 (r. 1413–1422)

One of the great English kings, Henry V consolidated England through his monarchy and his military abilities and would have unified the crowns of England and France had he lived a little over two months longer. Henry promoted the use of English as the language of government (instead of Norman French) and was the first king for over 300 years to correspond in English.

Born in Monmouth Castle, Wales to Henry Bolingbroke (later Henry IV) and

Left: Henry V. *History Department, UCL/Jo St. Mart*

his wife 16-year old Mary de Bohun. He was not at the time in line for the throne.

When his father was exiled in 1398 Richard II became the boy's unofficial protector (Richard and Bolingbroke were cousins and had been close as children), even accompanying Richard to Ireland. When his father became king, Henry became heir to the throne and was created Prince of Wales at his father's coronation. He was soon leading his father's army into Wales to fight Owain Glyndwr and then to defeat Harry Hotspur at the Battle of Shrewsbury (1403).

Henry IV died in March 1413 and Henry V immediately succeeded him and was crowned on April 9, 1413. His first publicly declared policy was to forget old emnities and unite the kingdom. Many nobles who had had lands and titles confiscated gradually had them returned and peace returned to the land, although Henry had to crush a rebellion in the name of Edmund Mortimer in 1415. Then Henry turned to France to fulfill his ambitions and recapture lost English lands. In August 1415 he set sail for Harfleur in Normandy which he captured. Then the army marched towards Calais but turned to fight the pursuing French army at Agincourt: there his exhausted but skilled longbow men fought to a decisive victory on October 25, 1415.

Right: 15th century French manuscript showing the Battle of Agincourt—a decisive English victory. *The Art Archive/Victoria and Albert Museum London/Harper Collins Publishers AA333929*

In the intervening period and throughout, the French and the church were constantly falling out with each other and swapping alliances. This disunited situation allowed Henry real advantage. In 1417 with the assistance of his brothers the dukes of Clarence, Bedford, and Gloucester he resumed his advance across France as they conquered lower Normandy and besieged Rouen. The city fell in January 1419 and retribution was taken against the Norman French. Henry then marched on Paris and was at the gates by August: the king and the French aristocracy still could not agree and many nobles allied themselves to Henry V as he captured Picardy and much of the Ile-de-France. Six months of negotiation resulted in the Treaty of Troyes (1420) and the potential alliance of the crowns of England and France through marriage.

In June 1420 he married Catherine of Valois, daughter of king Charles VI of France, and together they had one son, the future Henry VI. The marriage was part of the provisions of the Treaty of Troyes along with the repossession of the old Plantaganet territories of Normandy and Aquitaine. Another clause made Henry regent of France for King Charles' lifetime and then king after him, so England and France would be united under one crown. This never happened because Henry died first, just two months before Charles.

By the end of 1420 Henry returned to England and the following year went on royal progress with Catherine around the kingdom.

But in seven months he was back in France again, this time campaigning in the north. However, after victories at Dreux, Chartres, and Meaux Henry suddenly died aged 34 years old on August 31, 1422 at Bois de Vincennes, just outside Paris. The cause was probably dysentery caught during the siege of Meaux. He named his brother John of Lancaster, Duke of Bedford as regent of France for his infant son Henry VI–he was born while Henry was campaigning and he had never seen him. His body was taken back to London and buried in Westminster Abbey.

Henry VI
House of Lancaster
1422–1471 (r. 1422–1471)

As the English crown lost its French lands, England was riven with the Wars of the Roses, a nasty civil war over which side had the more legitimate claim to the throne. Henry VI presided over one of the bloodiest reigns in English history although he was not himself a military leader.

Henry was born at Windsor Castle the first son of Catherine of Valois while his father Henry V was campaigning in France. Within eight months his father was dead and Henry became king of England, then two months later when his grandfather Charles VI of France died, king of France. He was crowned king of England in 1429 in Westminster

Abbey and king of France in 1431 in Notre Dame, Paris.

Inevitably his reign started with a regency: His young French mother was not trusted so his uncle Humphrey, Duke of Gloucester was appointed Protector and head of the English regency council, and his other uncle John, Duke of Bedford regent for France. However when the latter died in 1435, Burgundy broke their alliance with England and English rule dissolved in France. This was the period of Joan of Arc and the Dauphin and French triumphs in the Hundred Years War as England lost ground, including Normandy in 1450.

In 1437 Henry came of age and took his place at the head of government but he lacked political judgement and allowed factionalism as his favorites exercised too much influence. The war party who wanted to regain lost French territories were ignored and Henry sought peace through a dynastic marriage to 16 year old Margaret of Anjou, the Queen of France's niece in 1445. Meanwhile his widowed mother Catherine had a longstanding relationship with Owen Tudor, resulting in at least six children and the eventual Tudor claim to the throne.

Henry's government was increasingly corrupt, extravagant, and unpopular especially with the loss of even more French territories. Then, in 1453 Henry had a complete mental breakdown on hearing of a bad English defeat in Aquitaine and Richard, Duke of York was made Protector of the Realm the following year. Even Henry's recovery in 1455 was not enough to stop the growing crisis between the Yorkists and Lancastrians which bloomed into a civil war known as the Wars of the Roses (the red rose symbolized Lancashire, and the white rose York). The Lancastrian cause was led by Margaret of Anjou as Henry was clearly incapable of leadership.

The Yorkist cause was led by the Duke of York who made his claim through Edward III's second (surviving) son via his mother; Henry VI's claim was through the third (surviving) son and his father. The matter was partially settled when the Duke of York was killed at the Battle of Wakefield in 1460, leaving his son Edward to take his place. The Lancastrians were beaten at the Battle of Towton (1461) and London opened the city gates to the victors. Henry and Margaret fled to Scotland as Edward of York was crowned Edward IV.

In 1465 Henry returned to reclaim

his throne but was instead captured and imprisoned in the Tower of London; however, the Earl of Warwick changed sides and restored Henry as king in 1470 and exiled Edward. The change was short-lived, following the Battle of Tewkesbury (1471) where his son Edward, Prince of Wales was killed, Henry was again captured and returned to the Tower where he was murdered on May 21, 1471. He was eventually buried at Windsor Castle.

Edward IV
House of York
1442–1483 (r. 1461–1483)

Born in Rouen in Normandy, Edward was the second son of Richard Plantagenet, Duke of York and Cecily Neville, a granddaughter of Edward III.

During the Wars of the Roses his father was the leading Yorkist until he was killed at the Battle of Wakefield in 1460 at which point Edward inherited his position (his older brother had died). With the support of Richard Neville, Earl Warwick ("the Kingmaker"), Edward was successful on the battlefield and following the conclusive Battle of Towton in 1461 the weak Lancastrian King Henry VI was deposed and Edward crowned Edward IV in Westminster Abbey.

The Earl of Warwick was determined to control the 19-year-old king and was working on a dynastic marriage for him when Edward secretly married his commoner sweetheart, Elizabeth Woodville and then promoted many of her relatives. The furious Earl then switched sides to support George, Duke of Clarence (Edward's younger brother) and lead a revolt against the king. When they were unsuccessful they fled to France to join Margaret of Anjou, Henry VI's vastly more capable wife. Together, with French support, they invaded England in September 1470 and briefly restored Henry to the throne of England.

Edward and his brother Richard, Duke of Gloucester, regrouped in Burgundy and returned in March 1471: they defeated Warwick and killed him at the Battle of Barnet, and then defeated the Lancastrians at the Battle of Tewkesbury in May. Henry was imprisoned and murdered.

The restored monarchy of Edward IV saw a reign when England was at peace and recovering from the bloody civil war.

Above: Edward IV at Calais after the battle of Lutford. *The Art Archive/Musée Thomas Dobrée, Nantes/Gianni Dagli Orti AA377098*

Above left: Portrait of Edward IV. *History Department, UCL via Jo St. Mart*

Trade was revived through new commercial treaties and government settled down. Edward largely used the income from his crown estates' profits to

pay the expenses of his government rather than request levies and subsidies from parliament. He tightly controlled the royal revenues and would often sit in person during court cases.

In 1475 Edward declared war on France and almost immediately concluded a peace with Louis XI. The Treaty of Picquigny saw Margaret of Anjou ransomed and pensions agreed with Edward and many of his nobles, but not his brother, who became Richard III.

With his health in decline Edward had time to consider his will: he named his 12-year-old son Edward his heir with his uncle Richard as protector. He died on April 9, 1483, aged 41 and was buried at Windsor Castle. His two young sons—Edward V and Richard—were left in the care of their uncle Richard, Duke of Gloucester. He placed them under protection in the Tower of London where they were almost certainly murdered, probably by Richard to stop them reappearing as pretenders to the crown.

With Elizabeth Woodville Edward had fathered ten legitimate children, seven daughters, and three sons. He also had a number of illegitimate children.

Parliament petitioned Richard to take the throne, he accepted and was crowned Richard III.

Edward V/Richard III
House of York
1452–1485 (r. 1483–1485)

Richard III is possibly the most controversial English monarch, his reputation shattered by the suspicion that he murdered his young nephews in the Tower of London. The Tudors liked to stigmatize him as Richard Crookback and claimed he had a withered arm, one short leg, and a hump—all of which are

Above: Edward V and Richard, Duke of York, in the Tower of London. *The Art Archive/Musée du Louvre Paris/Gianni Dagli Orti AA381029*

Left: Edward V. *via Jo St. Mart*

almost certainly lies created to blacken his character and justify their claim to the throne. During his short reign, the first laws written entirely in English were promulgated.

Born at Fotheringhay Castle in Northamptonshire in October 1452, Richard had a claim to the throne through both parents—Cecily Neville and Richard Plantagenet. He was their fourth and youngest surviving son and born just before the official outbreak of the Wars of the Roses in 1455; his early life was dominated by the conflict. In 1460 both his father and his older brother Edmund died at the Battle of Wakefield. In 1461, when his other brother Edward became Edward IV, he was rewarded for his loyalty and valor by being made Duke of Gloucester and appointed

married before. This meant the children were illegitimate and so Edward V was a usurper. On June 25 the lords and commoners agreed the argument and asked Richard, as true heir, to be their king. He was crowned in July at Westminster Abbey. The princes in the Tower were never heard from again and probably died in August: Richard was accused of murdering them.

Richard did what he could to reconcile with the Lancastrians but in October disquiet in the country erupted in rebellion started by the Duke of Buckingham–although this quickly collapsed it was clear that a good proportion of the gentry and aristocracy had ceased to support Richard.

The Lancastrian claimant to the throne, Henry Tudor, Earl of Richmond came out of exile to land an army in south Wales. Richard and his army rushed to meet them and a two-hour long battle at Bosworth Field ensued on August 22. The king had the bigger army but a number of his important supporters such as the Earl of Northumberland and the Earl of Derby, deserted him; even though his situation was dire, Richard refused to flee and was killed on the field of battle leaving Henry Tudor victorious. Richard was buried aged 32 in an unmarked grave in Leicester. He was the last of the Plantagenet dynasty and the final king of the House of York. Without a legitimate son, Richard had named his nephew John de la Pole, Earl of Lincoln (his older sister's son) as his heir.

Governor of the North (where he always remained popular). Richard went into exile with Edward to France before he was restored to the throne in 1471.

In July 1472 Richard married Anne Neville, the youngest daughter of the Earl of Warwick and a friend since childhood; they had one son who died aged nine. Richard also fathered a few illegitimate children.

On Edward IV's death in 1483 Richard was made Lord Protector of his young nephews, 12-year-old Edward V and 9-year-old Richard, Duke of York whom he lodged in the Tower of London for protection–the Princes in the Tower. Wanting the throne for himself Richard proclaimed that Edward IV's marriage to Elilzabeth Woodville was invalid because he had

Henry VII

House of Tudor
1457–1509 (r. 1485–1509)

Henry Tudor was born in Pembroke, Wales, the only son of Edmund Tudor – the eldest son of Catherine of Valois, the widow of Henry V, and her second husband Owen Tudor–and Lady Margaret Beaufort, a great grand-daughter of John of Gaunt (son of Edward III) and through whom Henry made his claim for the throne. Margaret was only 13 years old and seven months pregnant with Henry when Edmund Tudor died. Because of the ongoing Wars of the Roses Henry was brought up by his uncle Jasper Tudor, Duke of Bedford with whom he fled into 14 years of exile, first in Brittany then France.

In 1483 on Edward IV's death, Henry Tudor–with French support–became the leading Lancastrian claimant to the throne. To unite the warring houses of Lancaster and York he promised to marry Elizabeth of York, the eldest daughter of Edward IV. This pledge convinced many of the usurper Richard III's opponents to support the Tudor cause and when Henry and Jasper Tudor landed in Pembrokeshire, Wales they were well received. Henry quickly gathered a 5,000-strong army and marched across England to Leicestershire where he met the king's army. At the Battle of Bosworth Field, Richard III had the more soldiers but was deserted by some of his most prominent allies and he was killed on the battlefield. Henry Tudor was proclaimed Henry VII.

Above: Statue of Henry VII on Bath Abbey. *Bath Tourist Board via Jo St. Mart*

Because his assumption of the throne was controversial and his claim not the strongest, Henry VII still had to secure his position by unifying the warring factions involved in the Wars of the Roses. One of his first actions was to make good his promise and marry Elizabeth of York, so uniting the houses of Lancaster and York through their seven children. Their badge was the Tudor rose, a combination of the red and white roses of Lancaster and York.

Not everyone was convinced by the Tudor king and a number of revolts had to be quelled. Two of the most serious were pretenders to the throne: Perkin Warbeck claimed to be Richard, Duke of York, one of the lost princes in the Tower and Lambert Simnel claimed to be Edward, Earl of Warwick and son of the Duke of Clarence. Both were dealt with but not without trouble.

Henry was a born administrator and he set about regulating government, increasing administrative efficiency especially of taxation, promoting foreign trade, and strengthening the power of the monarchy–he is said to have personally examined the royal accounts almost every day, but he hardly ever called parliament, only seven in his 24-year reign. Medieval laws and ways of doing business were transformed into a more efficient and modern administration. Thanks to his stringencies the annual royal revenue rose from £52,000 to £142,000 by the time of his death. He also changed the royal council unto the Court of Star Chamber and charged it with maintaining the highest standards of justice.

So as to found a strong dynasty and keep the peace with his neighbors (wars cost huge amounts of money which Henry resented) he carefully married off his children: Margaret to James IV of Scotland, Mary to Louis XII of France,

Sawanach
GEORGIA
FLORIDA
S Auguſtinuſ
Prom Floridae
CUBA I

ENRICUS VII ANGLIAE REX JOANNEM
BOTAM ET SEBASTIANUM FILIUM
TRONOMIAE REIQ NAUTICAE PERI
SSIMOS ANNO MCCCCXCVI NAVA
HOS INSTITUIT SUIS LITTERISQUI
AM INVENIRENT QUAM ANIMO

and Arthur to Catherine of Aragon, daughter of Ferdinand II of Aragon and Isabella of Castile.

In 1502 Henry's oldest son and heir, Arthur, died in an epidemic aged 15; his wife Catherine also contracted the mystery illness but recovered. The following year Queen Elizabeth died in childbirth along with their baby, Katherine.

Henry died in April 1509, it was said of a broken heart. He left a full treasury, a powerful and wealthy throne, and a prosperous and largely peaceful kingdom. He was buried in Westminster Abbey.

Above: 1486 coin commemorating the marriage of Henry VII to Elizabeth of York. *The Art Archive AA347141*

Henry VIII
House of Tudor
1491–1547 (r. 1509–1547)

In the popular imagination Henry VIII is caricatured by his six wives: divorced, beheaded, died, divorced, beheaded, survived. But he was much more than this: in the early years of his reign he was a true Renaissance king, a sophisticated patron of the arts, very well educated, musical, intelligent, handsome, religious, athletic, and charming. It was only in his later years that his violent temper and single-minded desire for a male heir to establish the Tudor dynasty skewed his reason and almost wrecked the kingdom: throughout his reign he was feared and admired in almost equal parts.

Henry was born in Greenwich Palace, London, the third child of King Henry VII and Elizabeth of York. Until the sudden death of his older brother Arthur in 1502, Henry had probably been destined for the church and was largely ignored by his father. In his early years Henry was very religious and attended mass daily; he lived a sheltered life brought up quietly by his mother.

Henry VII died in 1509 and Henry VIII acceded to the throne uncontested, inheriting a stable kingdom and a full treasury. He also claimed his brother's widow, Catherine of Aragon, whom his father had retained in England because he did not want to return her huge dowry. She was some six years older than 17-year-old Henry but they were genuinely fond of each other and eager to marry which they did in June 1509: 13 days later they were both crowned at Westminster Abbey. Sadly Catherine lost all her babies except one, Mary born in 1516.

In 1513 Henry–with the promise of Spanish support–invaded France, where he won a victory at the Battle of the Spurs. In September back in England, the Scottish king James IV (also his brother-in-law) invaded northern England only to be soundly beaten at the Battle of Flodden Field in which King James was killed.

In the early 1520s across northwestern Europe Martin Luther and the Protestant Reformation were causing enormous trouble to the established Catholic Church. In 1521, horrified by the rise of Protestantism Henry wrote a riposte

Above: Henry VIII depicted in later life in his familiar pose.
Deborah Clague/Fotolia

Catherine of Aragon who was his aunt. Peace with France was signed in 1520 at the hugely extravagant festivities at the Field of the Cloth of Gold.

By 1525 Catherine was 40 years old and unlikely to produce an heir but the Tudor dynasty was still too new to risk passing to a female. Henry had fallen for Anne Boleyn, one of the queen's ladies in waiting, and decided that an annulment of his marriage from Catherine was the answer to his problem. If Pope Clement VII would annul his marriage (as popes had done before) on the grounds that she had been married to his brother then he would be free to marry Anne. Cardinal Wolsey was charged with the petition, and when he failed in May 1529, he was removed from office and arrested, but died before his trial. He was replaced by Sir Thomas More, but More resigned as Chancellor in 1532 when parliament passed acts recognizing Henry's supremacy over the church. Thomas Cromwell became Henry's new advisor and he used parliament and its anticlerical mood to agree the divorce. The wheels were set in motion for the English Reformation.

Henry took a real and intelligent interest in the matters of government; he personally interviewed foreign ambassadors and frequently attended the debates in the House of Lords. He loved the detail and avidly annotated state documents. His memory was phenomenal and he is said to have been able to remember names, dates, and details of all the papers he signed. However, his councillors' deliberations bored him and he would not read long documents and would postpone making crucial decisions as long as possible. He did appreciate that, as an island nation, England needed a strong navy and consequently increased it in size from five ships to 53.

In 1532 Pope Clement VII promoted Thomas Cranmer (the Boleyn family chaplain) to the position of Archbishop of Canterbury, unaware that he was prepared to declare Henry's marriage to Catherine of Aragon invalid (in 1533) and that she was no longer queen. Within a week Henry and the Protestant Anne Boleyn were married.

The Pope was furious and Henry was excommunicated: parliament reposted by denying all papal authority and announcing that the monarch (Henry) was the sole authority and the supreme head of the church in England. The English Protestant Reformation had started. Equally importantly parliament had been used as his instrument to force his will, but in turn had taken increased power to itself as

Assertio Septem Sacramentorum (Defence of the Seven Sacraments) supporting the position of the Roman Catholic Church and defending the supremacy of the pope. For this Pope Leo X gave Henry the title "Defender of the Faith"–it was revoked in 1530 but retained as a title by the English crown.

Henry had executed his father's two chief advisors, Sir Richard Empson and Edmund Dudley, and did not single out anyone himself until he appointed Thomas Wolsey, a humble butcher's son, as first his advisor and then his Lord Chancellor in 1515.

Through his own marriage and those of his sisters Henry was closely allied with the three of the most important crowns of Western Europe–France, Spain, and Scotland; he also had influence with Charles V, Holy Roman Emperor, through

an institution which was never relinquished.

Henry then ordered all members of the clergy to swear an oath of allegiance to him as supreme head of the church. Most of them complied, with the notable exception of Sir Thomas More, who was executed for treason in 1535. An enormous consequence of the English Reformation was the wholesale dissolution of the monasteries and abbeys. Monks and nuns were thrown out of their homes to become beggars, the vast monastery lands were distributed to Henry's favorites as gifts or sold, and most of the wealth of the monasteries—which was considerable—disappeared into the royal coffers. The buildings themselves were pillaged for stone. By 1540 all the monasteries had been dissolved.

Despite his second marriage no male heir appeared; instead, Anne Boleyn produced a baby girl (later Elizabeth I) in September 1533 and Anne was soon disgraced and beheaded in 1536 for treason on trumped up charges arranged by Thomas Cromwell, who in the process had become Henry's chief advisor. Her successor, Jane Seymour finally produced a male heir, Edward (later Edward VI) but she died 12 days later leaving a sickly baby. Each time Henry looked for a new wife elaborate plots were followed by the various political factions to catch the

Above left: Anne Boleyn was queen of England 1533–36. *The Art Archive/Galleria degli Uffizi Florence/Alfredo Dagli Orti AA346444*

Above: The young Henry VIII progressing to parliament three years into his reign. *The Art Archive/Bodleian Library Oxford/Ashmole Rolls 45r AA384035*

Right: Catherine of Aragon. *The Art Archive/Galleria degli Uffizi Florence/Alfredo Dagli Orti AA346595*

Left: Wolsey entertaining Henry VIII at Hampton Court. *The Art Archive/Victoria and Albert Museum London/Eileen Tweedy* AA337189

Cromwell, a Protestant himself, was pushing the king to make an important foreign Protestant marriage and arranged for his wedding to Anne of Cleves. This proved an immediate disaster as soon as Henry saw Anne: she was wise enough to accept a quick annulment, a pension, and a quiet life at Hever Castle in Kent. But Thomas Cromwell was never forgiven, he was made Earl of Essex in 1540 but within three months was arrested and executed. The day he was executed Henry married Catherine Howard: he was 50 years old, she between 15 and 20. The marriage was a disaster and ended within two years with Catherine accused of treason (really adultery) and beheaded.

Still looking for an heir and domestic happiness Henry married for the fifth and last time: his bride was a widow, Catherine Parr, who was in the household of his daughter Mary. By then he was ill and overweight and probably incapable of fathering another child. Parr's main contribution was to reconcile Henry with his daughters Mary and Elizabeth and place them back in line of succession after Edward with the Third Succession Act. This also provided for a Regency Council for Edward should Henry died before his majority.

Henry VIII died in the Palace of Whitehall, London on January 28, 1547 aged 55. He was buried at Windsor Castle beside Jane Seymour.

king's eye and secure preference, positions and influence for their family.

In 1536 a popular rising in York–the Pilgrimage of Grace–called for England's return to the Catholic fold, the dismissal of Cromwell, and the resolution of a number of specific social grievances. The stability of the kingdom was briefly shaken as the Pilgrimage of Grace threatened to become a widespread movement, but it was ruthlessly put down and the leaders executed. Between the years 1532–40 an unprecedented 330 political executions took place–a sure sign of the king's will to enforce changes: throughout his reign he is estimated to have executed around 72,000.

Catherine of Aragon died in 1536 when Anne was in the early stages of pregnancy. Around the same time Henry was jousting in a tournament when his horse fell on him and crushed

his leg, he may even have been close to death: the shock caused Anne to miscarry her 15 week old male baby. Henry never forgave her, he was now crippled and in constant pain and unable to take his usual vigorous exercise he quickly became huge and even more immobile. Anne was accused of bewitching the king, of adultery, incest and high treason: she was beheaded at a public execution at the Tower of London on May 19, 1536.

Ten days later Henry married Jane Seymour. At the same time Henry signed the Laws in Wales Act 1535 which united England and Wales into one unified nation. He also declared his daughters Mary and Elizabeth to be illegitimate and, therefore, not eligible to inherit the throne. Two years later Jane gave birth to the much desired son, Edward, but died following the difficult birth.

Edward VI

House of Tudor
1537–1553 (r. 1547–1553)

Edward was the much desired son of Henry VIII and his third wife, Jane Seymour. He was born at Hampton Court but his mother died of complications following childbirth a few days later.

Edward was never a robust child but he was clever and received a good education. When Henry VIII died in January 1547 he became undisputed king at the age of nine and was crowned at Westminster Abbey on February 20, 1547. Henry had intended a 12-man Regency Council to govern until Edward's majority at 18, but his uncle, Edward Seymour, instead assumed the role of Lord Protector of the Realm, the title Duke of Somerset, and wielded absolute power.

The Protestant Reformation had taken firm hold in much of Europe but despite Henry's break with the church England and Wales still largely remained sympathetic to the old ways–as had Henry despite pocketing the wealth of the church. The Duke of Somerset and Archbishop Cranmer were determined to establish the Reformation once and for all. Edward had received a Protestant education and completely supported their intent. In 1549 Cranmer produced the Book of Common Prayer and the Act of Uniformity was passed to enforce its use and English instead of Latin services in church.

People in Devon and Cornwall immediately revolted at the Prayer Book

while Kett's Rebellion in Norfolk also complained of social and economic injustices and especially against land enclosures. The latter was suppressed by John Dudley, Earl of Warwick. Heady with his success, Dudley managed to engineer Somerset's downfall in 1551, and him arrested and executed (1552). He assumed the role of protector (but not officially) and the title Duke of Northumberland. Meanwhile the French had declared war on England.

A new Prayer Book was published in 1552 as part of the renewed campaign to

Above: Edward VI as a child, painted by Hans Holbein the Younger. *The Art Archive/ National Gallery of Art Washington AA346917*

quicken the pace of the Reformation in England. Across the country religious imagery and statues were destroyed, altars became tables, stained glass destroyed, clergy were encouraged to marry, and an even tougher Act of Uniformity enforced the new religion.

Edward had never been robust and his illness was diagnosed as tuberculosis. His days, therefore, were

Above: Miniature portrait of Edward VI while Prince of Wales. *The Art Archive/Private Collection/Philip Mould AA527208*

Left: Edward VI painted just before he became king. *via Jo St. Mart*

numbered. Northumberland, anxious to firmly establish Protestantism across the country, had the devoutly Catholic Mary Tudor—next in line to the throne—declared illegitimate and instead had Edward confer his crown on Lady Jane Grey, a distant, Protestant descendant of Henry VIII who Northumberland quickly married to his own son, Lord Guilford Dudley.

Edward died on July 6, 1553 of tuberculosis aged 15. Northumberland had Jane declared queen but the overwhelming support across the country was for Mary.

Mary (Bloody Mary)

House of Tudor
1516–1558 (r. 1553–1558)

The only surviving daughter of Henry VIII and his first wife, Catherine of Aragon, was born at the Palace of Placentia, Greenwich in February 1516. A rather sickly child, she was very short-sighted and suffered from frequent headaches, but she was well educated and clever. She was named Princess of Wales and the heir to the throne by her doting father until her life changed completely. Her father became infatuated with and married Anne Boleyn and she and her mother were separated: they both refused to renounce their Catholic faith.

Her parents finally divorced in 1531 when Mary was 17. She was declared illegitimate, demoted to "Lady Mary," removed from the succession, banished from court, lost her servants, and forced to served her half-sister Elizabeth. Five years later Catherine of Aragon died of cancer and Mary, forbidden to go to her funeral, was forced to sign a submission rejecting the pope's authority, accepting that her parents had never married and that, therefore, she was a bastard.

In 1543 Henry's sixth wife Catherine Parr worked on the old king to reunite his family, and the following year in the Third Succession Act both Mary and Elizabeth were restored to their position in the line of succession to the throne.

Right: Princess Mary after she was allowed to return to court in 1544. She became Queen Mary in 1553. *via Jo St. Mart*

At the age of 38 Mary married the much younger Philip of Spain in July 1554. She was in love; he was marrying for political reasons. Although he was styled King of England, his powers were very limited. The queen thought herself pregnant but it proved false and Philip returned to Spain leaving her desolate; he became Philip II of Spain on his father's abdication in 1556.

All Edward's religious laws were repealed in the first parliament and then all of Henry VIII's in successive parliaments. In 1555 Mary re-enacted the statute of de heretico comburendo allowing heretics to be burned at the stake to cleanse their souls: one of the first to suffer was Thomas Cranmer, who had made her parents' divorce possible. Some 300 or so others followed in the "Marian Persecutions."

Philip of Spain briefly returned to Mary in 1557 and talked her into a war against France. It did not go well and the last English enclave on French soil – the port of Calais–fell to the French in January 1558.

After another false pregnancy (it turned out to be a tumor), Philip persuaded Mary to name her sister Elizabeth as successor and tried to get her married to a Spaniard. Elizabeth refused and Mary would not force her.

In November 1558 Mary died aged 42, probably of ovarian cancer.

Above left: Philip II of Spain with Mary I of England, seen in 1554, the year they married. *Getty Images*

Right: Portrait of Mary I by Antonis Moro in 1554. *The Art Archive/Museo del Prado Madrid AA347661*

Assailed on all sides to renounce her faith, her prime supporter was Charles V of Spain. Although at times close to her half-brother Edward, he was persuaded on his deathbed to disinherit Mary in favor of the Protestant Lady Jane Grey. But public support was for Mary and she became queen in August 1553.

Mary's aim was to restore the old religion to the country and overturn the Protestant reforms. To help her she chose to marry her Catholic cousin Philip of Spain, son of Emperor Charles V. But the choice of foreign prince was greatly unpopular with her subjects and rebellion erupted led by Thomas Wyatt. Princess Elizabeth was arrested and sent to the Tower for two months for being suspected of involvement in the plot.

Elizabeth I
House of Tudor
1583–1603 (r. 1558–1603)

Born at Greenwich Palace Elizabeth was the only child of Henry VIII and his second wife, Anne Boleyn. Her mother was executed when she was only 32 months old. Elizabeth was declared illegitimate and removed from court as her father could not bear to see her; nevertheless she was extremely well educated. Elizabeth returned to court (as did her half-sister Mary) when her stepmother Catherine Parr became queen. She lived in the Parr household for a time after Henry VIII died (when Elizabeth was 13 years old). But she was continually surrounded by plots to put her onto or remove her from contention for the throne; similarly numerous attempts were made to marry her for her position. Her sister Mary even had her imprisoned in the Tower for two months after she was implicated in the Wyatt Rebellion. She was then allowed to go to Hatfield under semi-house arrest. She was there when she heard that she had become queen on November 17, 1558: she was 25.

Left: *Eliza Triumphans* by William Rodgers, 1589. *The Art Archive AA350155*

Below: Elizabeth I at prayer, on a frontispiece painting to *Christian Prayers and Meditations*, 1569. *The Art Archive AA346913*

Elizabeth I was crowned amid great celebrations and festivities at Westminster Abbey in January 1559. She quickly made it clear that she would support the establishment of an English Protestant church—but pragmatic compromises were made so Catholics would not be alienated by the new monarchy and the heresy laws were repealed.

Throughout her reign Elizabeth was the target of many marriage proposals, even Philip II of Spain, her sister Mary's widower, attempted to persuade her to marry him, but Elizabeth although encouraging suitors never agreed to marriage. Instead Elizabeth used her unmarried status as a lure to leverage her domestic and foreign policies. She knew

a foreign prince would be unpopular—and if she married a French prince there would immediately be war with Spain. Similarly, by marrying an Englishman she would only faction the country along regional and religious lines. Instead she became the Virgin Queen married to her country.

In 1562 Elizabeth survived a bout of smallpox at the cost of scarred skin and the loss of half her hair: from then on she took to wearing wigs and thick makeup.

One of the greatest threats to Elizabeth's reign was from her cousin Mary Queen of Scots who, as the Catholic candidate, was supported by the French. Deeply unpopular and with her life in danger from the Protestants in Scotland, Mary fled to England for protection, but instead was taken under house arrest for 19 years. The plots around Mary swirled continuously and with her probable involvement in the Babington Plot (1586) she became too dangerous to live and Elizabeth finally, reluctantly, signed her death warrant in February 1587.

Above: Elizabeth I of England by an unknown artist. *The Art Archive/Galleria degli Uffizi Florence/Alfredo Dagli Orti AA346889*

Left: Elizabeth I carefully cultivated her image through her magnificent costumes and jewelery and paintings such as this. *The Art Archive/Palazzo Pitti Florence/Alfredo Dagli Orti AA357524*

By and large a popular monarch, Elizabeth established a remarkable stability and religious compromise at a time when civil war could easily have erupted. To reinforce her government she regularly showed herself to her people around the country on regional "progresses" of which she made at least 25 during her reign. These had the secondary attraction of reducing the costs of running the court as others had the "honor" of putting up the royal household for a period.

In 1570 the pope issued as papal bull releasing Elizabeth's subjects from their allegiance; in response she passed fierce laws against Roman Catholics as plots against her life were uncovered. She found parliament difficult and largely uncooperative, and only called the assembly 16 times during her reign. However, she did not try to alter parliament's right's although she vetoed any legislation of which she did not

approve. Instead she ruled by using a trusted group of good councillors and advisors, chief of whom was William Cecil, Baron Burghley.

Spain wanted to control England and with no prospect of a marriage with Elizabeth, the Spanish Armada of around 130 galleons was assembled and sent to England with the pope's blessing. Philip intended to re-establish Catholicism and become king as the previous monarch's husband gave him a sound claim. But Elizabeth's navy and favorable winds dispersed the Spanish and the immediate threat of conquest. English navigators and explorers such as Sir Francis Drake sailed the seas to North America where they tried to establish a colony; Virginia was named for Elizabeth.

Throughout the 1590s England suffered from severe economic depression, poor harvests, and high prices and the countryside was especially badly affected. The draining costs of conflicts with Spain, France, and Ireland affected the economy and pushed taxation higher, and Elizabeth's personal popularity suffered.

Elizabeth's religious views are not known, and her actions do not reveal them. Her reign did not see the excesses of the Marian Persecutions, although there were burnings. She had to ensure that her Protestant subjects were kept happy, but her reign saw more tolerant attitudes.

Left: The "Darnley Portrait" painted by an unknown artist in 1575. The queen probably posed for the painting and it is regarded as the definitive image of her. *via Jo St. Mart*

Above: The "Armada Portrait" so called because it was painted in 1588. *The Art Archive/Private Collection/Philip Mould AA525580*

Left: Elizabeth I in 1599. *Westminster Council/ Jo St. Mart*

In the late 1590s the matter of succession became ever more pressing with Elizabeth refusing to name her successor, leaving her new advisor, Robert Cecil (son of her most trusted advisor Burghley) to work in secret to secure a smooth transfer of power. Cecil worked with King James VI of Scotland, whose claim was strong but not authorized by Henry VIII's will; he was advised to placate Elizabeth.

Elizabeth died after a six-month melancholic illness (a number of her close friends had died) at Richmond Palace on March 24, 1603. With her ended the Tudor dynasty. She was buried in Westminster Abbey beside her sister Mary.

James I (and VI of Scotland)

House of Stuart
1566–1625 (r. 1567–1625 in Scotland;
1603–1625 in England)

The first of the Stuart kings of England was born in Edinburgh Castle the son of Mary, Queen of Scots, and Lord Darnley who was murdered within a year of his birth. Queen Elizabeth of England was his godmother. Catholic Mary, Queen of Scots was implicated in the murder, and her Protestant enemies used the suspicion to force her to abdicate in favor of her 13-month-old son James, he was then brought up as a member of the Protestant church of Scotland and never saw his mother again. Throughout his minority James was left to the care of various regents as Scotland survived the threat of civil war caused by religious differences; the official religion of Scotland was Presbyterianism and Roman Catholicism was suppressed. James actively became king of Scotland in 1581.

James claimed the crown of England and Wales through Henry VII's daughter, Margaret (his great grandmother), and the Treaty of Berwick which both he and Elizabeth I signed in 1586. The treaty pledged allegiance, non-aggression, and mutual help against invasion.

James had been king of Scotland for 36 years before becoming king of England. He had for some time been in secret contact with Elizabeth's most trusted advisor, Robert Cecil, agreeing on various details for the coming reign, so that when Elizabeth died James was immediately proclaimed king in both England and Scotland. James moved south to London where he was received with great enthusiasm–everyone was relieved after years of worry that the empty throne would trigger civil

Top left: An engraving of James I of England and VI of Scotland and his consort Anne of Denmark. *via Jo St. Mart*

Left: 17th century coins: from the reign of King James I, the Commonwealth, and King Charles II. *The Art Archive/British Museum/ Eileen Tweedy AA328363*

Right: Flemish portrait of James I. *The Art Archive/Private Collection Italy/ Gianni Dagli Orti AA368562*

war or invasion. However, even more than Elizabeth, James believed in the divine right of kings and his right to behave as an absolute monarch, additionally he did not have much regard for parliaments. Unsurprisingly, it was not long before James was viewed with enormous suspicion and not just because he was a foreigner. The Gunpowder Plot of 1605 was only one of many attempts on the life of King James. The would-be assassins were prepared to blow up the full session of parliament along with the king; they were betrayed and ultimately met a horrible death, celebrated annually ever since—mandatory until 1859 .

James's personal aim was to establish the union of the crowns of England and Scotland: one monarch, one parliament, one law—although this was not popular on either side of the border. One of his greatest achievements was to commission a new version of the bible, known as the King James Bible, which became the standard text for over 250 years.

In 1589 James married Anne of Denmark and together they had nine children only three of which survived childhood. His son and heir, Prince Henry, died (probably from typhoid) in 1612 throwing James into prolonged and deep depression, made only worse by the death of his wife Anne in 1619.

James died age 58 in March 1625 and was buried at Westminster Abbey.

Left: James I of England and VI of Scotland. *The Art Archive/Palazzo Pitti Florence/Alfredo Dagli Orti AA357063*

Above: James I wearing the chivalric Order of the Garter which bears the inscription *Honi soit qui mal y pense*—"evil be to him who evil thinks." *The Art Archive/Museo del Prado Madrid/Alfredo Dagli Orti AA347298*

Charles I
House of Stuart
1600–1649 (r. 1625–1649)

The second son of James VI of Scotland and Anne of Denmark, Charles was born at Dunfermline Palace in Fife, Scotland in November 1600. He became the heir to the crowns of England and Scotland on the death of his older brother Henry in 1612. When James I became senile in his final years, Charles and his father's favorite, George Villiers, Duke of Buckingham, effectively ruled in his place.

Charles I became king on the death of his father in 1625 and three months later–despite all popular and parliamentary advice to the contrary–he married Henrietta Maria of France (sister

Below: Charles I from an engraving by Robert Peake, c. 1760. *The Art Archive AA350621*

Charles was deeply religious, following a High Anglican form of worship, while Henrietta Maria was a Catholic–both made people uneasy and suspicious, especially in Puritan Scotland and increasingly so in England. His court was highly cultivated and extravagant, the arts were celebrated, and the royal picture collection greatly increased, racking up the crown debts.

Religion and foreign policy dominated Charles' reign and the conflict between the king's right to rule as opposed to parliament's authority. The Thirty Years War–a bitter conflict between Catholic and Protestant countries–was raging across western Europe. Charles wanted to intervene against Spain but parliament would not fund sufficient money. The incompetent Buckingham went to war anyway while Charles attempted to levy taxes without parliamentary consent. Buckingham was assassinated in 1628 while under impeachment and the war against Spain effectively ended. 1629 saw the start of the Eleven Years' Tyranny (or Personal Rule)–the ultimate exercise of absolute authority–when Charles I ruled without parliament (as earlier monarchs had done) using ancient and obsolete laws and precedents to raise revenue.

In 1639 the First Bishops' War broke out in Scotland as Charles attempted to enforce the use of a more Anglican prayer book, but he was forced into a humiliating truce at the Treaty of Ripon which precipitated a financial and military crisis and made necessary the recall of parliament in April 1640 and ended the era of personal rule. Charles was given no choice but to revoke a

Above: Charles I and his second son James, Duke of York (later James II), in 1647. *via Jo St. Mart*

Left: Charles I, the only British monarch to have been deposed and executed by parliament. *The Art Archive/Private Collection/Philip Mould AA532326*

of Louis XIII): together they produced six children who lived beyond infants.

Charles was crowned at Westminster Abbey in February 1626. Like his father he believed in the Divine Right of Kings, but unlike him Charles would neither compromise nor listen to the opinions of others, and is reported to have said, "Kings are not bound to give an account of their actions but to God alone."

number of assumed powers but conflicts over money, foreign wars, and religion continued and civil war became inevitable.

Charles fled to Oxford where he set up his court and government over north, west, and southwest England: Parliament controlled London, the south, and East Anglia, the army and, crucially, the navy. Civil war officially started at the Battle of Edgehill in October 1642. Battles ebbed and flowed until Charles fled to Scotland but after nine months the Presbyterians gave him back to the English Parliamentarians in 1647 and he was imprisoned.

In July 1648 the Second Civil War opened at Charles' insigation when the Royalists started uprisings around the country, Wales rebelled, and Scotland invaded. However the Parliamentarians successfully put down the rebellions and in January 1649 the Rump Parliament passed an Act to try Charles for high treason. Charles refused to acknowledge the authority of the court but was found guilty and 59 Commissioners signed his death warrant in January 1649. Three days later Charles was publicly beheaded in front of the Banqueting Hall in Whitehall on January 30, 1649. His head was sewn back onto his body which was buried at Windsor Castle.

On February 7, 1649 the position of king was formally abolished.

Right: Charles II crowned by the Marquess of Argyll at Scone, 1651, with Scotland allegorically presenting a pistol, and Ireland adjusting his armor. *The Art Archive AA350587*

Charles II
House of Stuart
1630–1685 (r. 1660–1685)

The reign of Charles II followed the Interregnum–the period when first Oliver and then Richard Cromwell governed England.

Charles was born in London at St. James's Palace, London, the son of Charles I and Henrietta Maria of France. During the English civil war, aged 14, he campaigned alongside his father until he was sent abroad for his own safety. In Edinburgh, a little over a month after his father's execution on February 5, 1649, the Scottish

Parliament declared Charles King of Scotland and he was crowned on January 1, 1651. For this he had to accept certain conditions: namely introduce, support, and guarantee Presbyterian church governance over Britain as signed in the Solemn League and Covenant–this won him the crown in Scotland but lost him support in England. Charles and his largely Scottish royalist army moved south into England where they met with Cromwell's forces at the Battle of Worcester in September 1651. The invaders were defeated and after six weeks of near capture (including hiding in an oak tree) Charles escaped to Normandy and Oliver Cromwell became Lord Protector of England,

Scotland, and Ireland. Charles remained in exile for nine years: in 1658 Cromwell died and was succeeded by his son Richard, but he only lasted a year and the Protectorate was abolished. The new Convention Parliament, despite attempts at packing it, turned out to be almost equally divided between Royalists and Parliamentarians. Hearing of the Declaration of Breda (April 1660) in which Charles laid out his conditions for accepting the English throne, and crucially his intention to pardon most of his father's enemies, Charles was invited to take the throne.

Charles arrived back in England and entered London on May 29, 1660, his 30th birthday. On April 23, at Westminster Abbey, Charles II was crowned King of England and Ireland. This period became known as the Restoration. Charles and Parliament granted an amnesty to Cromwell's supporters with the exception of 50 people: they were tried, some were excluded from office, some got life imprisonment, and nine regicides were executed. Oliver Cromwell's body was removed from Westminster Abbey, his body hung in chains at Tyburn, and his severed head displayed on a pole outside Westminster Abbey for 24 years.

The new Cavalier Parliament passed a series of acts which together became known as the Clarendon Code. This enacted a number of anti-Puritan laws and re-established the position and influence of the Church of England.

Left: Contemporary mezzotint of Charles II. *via Jo St. Mart*

In 1662 Charles married Catherine of Braganza, a Portugese Roman Catholic princess, she brought a dowry which included the important trading port cities of Tangier and Bombay. They did not have children together but Charles notoriously had numerous mistresses–including Nell Gwyn–and 12 illegitimate children.

In late summer and fall 1665 the Great Plague of London killed up to 100,000 people, about a fifth of the population. Anyone with money, including the king and his court, fled to the country. Charles moved to Salisbury and parliament to Oxford. The plague ended in the flames of the Great Fire of London in September 1666 in which even St. Paul's Cathedral was consumed.

By 1669 it was obvious that the unfortunate queen could not produce a living baby, (and Charles refused to remarry) so the heir presumptive became James, Duke of York, Charles' unpopular Catholic brother. To make this acceptable it was agreed that James' daughter Mary would marry the Protestant William of Orange. Personally Charles favored appeasement and compromise when it came to religion but was thwarted by Parliament in 1672 when he tried to introduce religious freedom with the Royal Declaration of Indulgence.

Religion was still the prime motivator for domestic and foreign policy and this was reflected on the world stage as other European countries struggled to reach their own accord within their

Right: Charles II wearing the robes of the Order of the Garter. *via Jo St. Mart*

borders and with their neighbors. From the 1650s England and the Dutch were involved in a series of wars as the English tried to subvert and claim Dutch markets and sources of world trade: one consequence was the English capture of the Dutch settlement of New Amsterdam which they renamed New York after James, Duke of York, Charles' brother. Alliances changed with the times but all wars cost money which parliament was reluctant to concede. This forced Charles to make peace in 1674.

In 1679 Titus Oates announced the existence of a "Popish Plot" and a Roman Catholic scheme to assassinate the king–this provoked anti-Catholic hysteria and the Exclusion Bill by which parliament tried to remove James, Duke of York from the line of succession. In response rival sides emerged: the pro-exclusion Whig party and the anti-exclusion Tory party, to which Charles allied himself. Following the Exclusion Crisis Charles dissolved his final parliament in 1679 and ruled by himself until his death.

Charles died in February 1685 following an apoplectic fit aged 54. He converted to Catholicism on his deathbed and was buried in Westminster Abbey.

Left: Charles II became known as the "Merry Monarch." *The Art Archive/Garrick Club AA340040*

Right: Portrait of James II in his garter robes. *Bridgeman Art Library/Getty Images 57315071*

James II
House of Stuart
1633–1701 (r. 1685–1688)

Born the third son of Charles I and Henrietta Maria of France at St. James's Palace, London, James spent his youth in exile in France and served in the French army until changing to fight with the Spanish. When his brother Charles became king, James became heir presumptive .

From the start James' love life was complicated: he had many lovers and fathered many children. Against all advice in 1660 he secretly married Anne Hyde, a commoner, who was carrying his child: over the years they lost numerous children, only two daughters survived to adulthood but the couple

remained devoted despite James' numerous mistresses. In about 1668 James and Anne secretly converted to Catholicism. Anne died in 1671.

James became his brother's Lord High Admiral, a lucrative and important post, and commanded the Royal Navy in action against the Dutch. But in 1673 he gave up the post when required to swear the Test Act–basically accepting the Church of England–and his conversion to Catholicism became generally known. In 1673 James married for the second time, his bride was the 15-year-old Mary of Modena, an Italian Catholic princess: they had two sons and five daughters.

By the 1670s it was apparent that James was Charles' successor; to temper the fears James finally consented to his daughter Mary's (raised as a Protestant) marriage to his nephew, the Protestant William, Prince of Orange. Anti-Catholics meanwhile tried to exclude James from the succession altogether in favor of James, Duke of Monmouth, Charles' illegitimate son.

Charles II died in 1685 making brother James king–James II in England and James VII in Scotland–aged 51. His accession was undisputed, the virulent anti-Catholic feeling had subsided somewhat following plots to return the Puritan Commonwealth.

James was crowned at Westminster Abbey in April 1685. He retained most of Charles' advisors and officers and

Left: James II's mausoleum in the Eglise de Saint Germain, Saint Germain-en-Laye, France. *The Art Archive/Gianni Dagli Orti AA379876*

immediately called parliament, but he soon faced a double-pronged rebellion, from his nephew, the Duke of Monmouth in the south of England and the Earl of Argyll in Scotland, both funded by the Netherlands. Both rebellions failed and both leaders were executed. Across the west of England a series of treason trails known as the Bloody Assizes meted out rough justice to the rebels. The upshot of the rebellions was that James created a large standing army and attempted to introduce religious equality laws. Parliament objected to his use of Catholic commanders and was dismissed never to be recalled in James II's reign.

In 1687 James issued the Declaration of Indulgence in an attempt to promote religious tolerance of Catholics and non-conformists, but instead this had the effect of escalating religious tension. James continued to promote Catholics to high office in government, the military, and educational institutions, but trouble escalated when he fathered a Catholic son, James Francis Edward Stuart (later the Old Pretender), on June 10, 1688. On June 30 a group of Protestant nobles–later known as the Immortal Seven–invited William of Orange to invade England and take the throne. William arrived in November and crucially the Army and Navy, as well as a number of nobles, swapped allegiance to join him. By December James had lost so much ground that he attempted to flee to France. He was captured in Kent before being allowed to escape to refuge with his cousin Louis XIV who gave him a palace at Saint-Germain-en-Laye and a pension. Parliament decided that James had abdicated by fleeing and by

dropping the Great Seal of the Realm into the Thames. They declared his daughter Mary queen and her husband William king. They also delared that from then on no Catholic could ascend the throne nor any member of the royal family marry one, a ruling that still applies today.

James attempted to retake the throne with a French army in Ireland, but lost heavily at the Battle of the Boyne in 1690. He died in 1701 at Saint-Germain-en-Laye and was buried in Paris.

Below: William, Prince of Orange, as a boy, c. 1665. *The Art Archive/Musée des Beaux Arts Lyon/Gianni Dagli Orti AA378689*

William III and Mary II
House of Stuart
William 1650–1702 (r. 1689–1702)
Mary 1662–1694 (1689–1694)

Mary was the daughter of James II and his first wife, Anne Hyde, and was born at St. James's Palace; she was brought up as an Anglican on Charles II's orders. Mary was bethrothed, against her father's wishes, to her first cousin the Protestant William, Prince of Orange. He was born in The Hague, the posthumous son of William II of Nassau and Mary Stuart, the eldest daughter of

WILLIAM III
OF ORANGE
KING OF GREAT BRITAIN

Charles I. By the age of nine he was an orphan. They married in 1677 in London when William was 27 and Mary 15, and moved to the Netherlands to live: to Mary's enduring sorrow their union was childless.

In June 1688 William was formally asked in secret (as already negotiated) by the Immortal Seven to invade England with his army where he would be greeted by a spontaneous popular uprising which would put the pair of them on the throne. Originally the crown was only offered to Mary but William refused to cooperate until he was given parity with her. The army landed in Torbay on November 5 and was quickly joined by the English Navy and Army. When James fled to France parliament declared him to have abdicated, so they offered the crown to William and Mary as joint sovereigns. They were crowned in Westminster Abbey on April 11, 1689, the same day they were offered the Scottish crown. In all this became known as The Glorious Revolution.

In December 1689 the Bill of Rights was passed by parliament. This greatly limited the powers of the sovereign, many of which could only be used through and with the consent of parliament. Moreover, from then on the sovereign was financially dependent on parliament.

From 1690 Mary administered the government as William fought abroad, initially against the Jacobites in Ireland and then against French expansionism in the Netherlands. She died of smallpox aged 32 in December 1694 at Kensington Palace and was buried at Westminster Abbey. William continued to rule alone but was not generally

Above: Coinage from the reign of William and Mary. *via Jo St. Mart*

Left: Statue of William III outside Kensington Palace, London. *Fotolia*

Right: William III and his wife Mary c.1639. *Hulton Archive/Getty Images 2637782*

popular especially with regard to his Dutch advisors. Without an heir parliament passed the Act of Settlement (1701) to ensure the Protestant succession, Anne was the next in line but only had one sickly child despite 17 pregnancies, so the honor passed to Sophia, Electress of Hanover.

William III died in 1702 of pneumonia after falling off his horse and breaking his collarbone at Hampton Court and the throne passed to Mary's sister Anne. He was buried in Westminster Abbey beside Mary.

Anne

House of Stuart
1665–1714 (r. 1702–1714)

Like her sister Mary II, Anne was born at St. James's Palace, London, the daughter of James II and his first wife, Anne Hyde ,and was raised as an Anglican.

In July 1683 Anne married George, Prince of Denmark, and between 1683 and 1700 had around 18 pregnancies, but only one son survived infancy, William, Duke of Gloucester. He died age 11 in 1700 and a succession crisis became apparent as the next heir was either the exiled James II or his son James Stuart. The Act of Settlement was hastily enacted securing the Protestant succession.

Anne succeeded her sister Mary and brother-in-law William of Orange to the throne in March 1702 because they had no direct heirs, becoming in the process the last of the Stuart kings.

Within months the War of the Spanish Succession started with England taking the side of Archduke Charles as the heir to the Spanish throne. The war and its consequences dominated England's foreign and domestic policy for almost her entire reign. Anne made her husband George, Lord High Admiral, put him in charge of the Royal Navy and gave Lord Marlborough control of the army.

Party political affiliations came to the fore during Anne's reign: the Tories supported strong monarchy and the Anglican Church of England, while the Whigs spoke for limited monarchy and religious dissenters.

In the matter of the succession England and Scotland diverged: the English Parliament declared the crown should go to the nearest royal Protestant relative, Sophia, Electress of Hanover, while the Scots on the whole preferred the exiled Catholic James Stuart. On May 1, 1707, after months of angry argument the two parliaments signed the Acts of Union 1707 creating the Kingdom of Great Britain and merged as one parliament sitting in Westminster, London: they also shared a common coinage and flag. However, religion was excepted, Scotland would retain the Church of Scotland plus its own legal and educational systems; broadly the same demarcations remain today. Separately, Anne was Queen of Ireland.

In 1708 Prince George of Denmark died at Windsor leaving Anne desolate but the Whigs delighted. A struggle for power and precedence followed as the Whigs tried to gain control of government with the active help of the Duchess of Marlborough guiding the grieving queen. Queen Anne had been dominated for 20 years or so by this strong-minded friend, Sarah Jennings Churchill (they had met as children in 1673), whose husband John Churchill became the Duke of Marlborough and a national hero for his military victories at Blenheim, Ramilies, Oudenarde, and Malplaquet. It was Sarah who got Anne to support William of Orange rather than her father James II in 1688. Always anxious to promote her Whig friends, Sarah eventually went too far and was dismissed along with her husband from favor and court.

The War of Spanish Succession continued with ever-mounting costs and consequent unpopularity for it and the Whig party. The general election of 1710 returned a Tory majority and they initially attempted to reach a peace before events changed their minds. With the arguments raging, Anne created 12 new peers to outnumber the Tory majority in the House of Lords which won the majority vote for peace and ended Britain's involvement in foreign war.

Anne died from a side effect of gout in August 1714 and was buried in Westminster Abbey. Thanks to the Act of Settlement her successor was Georg Ludwig, Elector of Hanover (Sophia's son) rather than any of the 56 Catholic successors who had a much stronger claim.

Left: Statue of Queen Anne outside St. Paul's Cathedral, London. *Westminster Council via Jo St. Mart*

Right: Anne in her ermine-trimmed coronation robes. *Hulton Archive/Getty Images 51242191*

George I
House of Hanover
1660–1727 (r. 1714–1727)

Born in Osnabrück, Lower Saxony, which was part of the Holy Roman Empire, George Ludwig was the son of Ernest Augustus, Duke of Brunswick-Lüneburg, and Sophia, the granddaughter of James I of England. When he was 15 his father took him campaigning in the Franco-Dutch War to familiarize him with military affairs.

In 1682 George married his first cousin, Sophia Dorothea, unifying the principalities of Hanover and Celle: together they had two children but their marriage was eventually dissolved on the grounds of infidelity and she was imprisoned in the Castle of Ahlden at the age of 28 until her death in 1726. George never married again and instead made no attempt to hide his many mistresses.

In 1698 George's father died leaving him with almost all his territories and titles, in particular Duke of Brunswick-Lüneburg and also Prince-Elector of the Holy Roman Empire. Soon after the English parliament passed the Act of Settlement allowing only Protestants to inherit and putting his mother in direct line to the throne of England. In 1705 George's last uncle died leaving him with Lüneberg-Grubenhagen, the same year Queen Anne made him a British citizen and rewarded him with numerous titles. When the War of Spanish Succession broke out, the Holy Roman Empire opposed the French claim to Spain and George helped by invading pro-French Brunswick-Wolfenbüttel: for his efforts George was rewarded with Saxony-Lauenburg.

In 1714 Queen Anne died and 54-year-old George was given the throne and crowned at Westminster Abbey in October. From then on George spent most of his time in England, though he returned to Hanover every couple of years. In his absence power was given to a Regency Council,

Left: George I and family. *The Art Archive/Royal Naval College Greenwich /Eileen Tweedy AA337126*

Above right: James III—the Old Pretender—son of James II. *The Art Archive/San Carlos Museum Mexico City/Gianni Dagli Orti AA382055*

not George, Prince of Wales; the latter was continually suspected, correctly, of engaging in political intrigue as opposition to the king naturally gravitated to the prince: the pair greatly disliked each other.

The Jacobite Rebellion of 1715 attempted to put James Stuart (the "Old Pretender")–arguably the true king–on the throne. Always stronger in Scotland, the Jacobites nevertheless failed and James spent the remainder of his life in exile in Rome.

George was not much interested in internal British politics which allowed the drift of increasing power to politicians such as Sir Robert Walpole, instead George actively engaged in foreign policy; especially with regard to Hanover where he was still an absolute monarch.

On his sixth trip home to Hamburg in June 1727 George suffered a stroke and died soon after; he was aged 66. He was buried at Leineschloss, his ancestral home. George had not been a particularly popular king, partly because he was considered too German and because of the misconception that he could not speak English, but for the majority he was better than James Stuart, the Catholic alternative.

Above: George I became the first Hanoverian king of Great Britain. *The Art Archive/Handel Museum Halle/Alfredo Dagli Orti AA347028*

Right: George I was disliked because he could not speak English, but tolerated because he wasn't Catholic. *The Art Archive/Musée du Château de Versailles/Gianni Dagli Orti AA363356*

George II

House of Hanover
1683–1760 (r. 1727–1760)

Born in Hanover, Georg August was the last British monarch born outside Britain. His father, George Ludwig, was Prince of Brunswick-Lüneburg when he was born, but George I after 1714. His mother Sophia of Celle was divorced in 1694 and never saw her son again.

Although she had a number of suitors Margravine Caroline of Brandenburg-Ansbach married George in August 1705 in Hanover and together they had eight children. Throughout their marriage George kept two mistress (a convention of the time) and when Queen Caroline died in November 1737 George refused to remarry preferring a string of mistresses.

When his father became George I in 1714 he became Prince of Wales. The pair actively and openly detested each other. When his son George William was christened in 1717, a quarrel at the baptism was so bad that the king had him temporarily arrested and then banished from his home at St. James's Palace and excluded from all public ceremonies.

From his new London home Leicester House, George orchestrated opposition against his father. One of his allies was the Whig party leader Sir Robert Walpole who rose to an almost unassailable position of political power after mitigating the disastrous financial effects of the economic disaster known as the South Sea Bubble when the economy, the royal purse, and many aristocrats and nobles lost catastrophic amounts of money. In the process Walpole changed sides to join the king's government, something the prince found difficult to forgive.

George II was crowned at Westminster Abbey in October 1727; against all public expectation he retained Walpole as his prime minister. In turn he, too, had problems with his eldest son, Friedrich Ludwig, Prince of Wales and even banished him and his new wife from court in 1737.

In 1739, against all his ministers' advice, George entered into war against Spain in the War of Jenkins' Ear which, on the death of Charles VI, Holy Roman Emperor, turned into the War of the Austrian Succession. George was ostensibly supporting Maria Theresa's right to inherit her father's throne against French pretensions, but in reality–and as his public suspected–he was more interested in protecting his German possessions. George became the last British king (at the age of 60) to lead his troops into battle at Dettingen in 1743. In retaliation the French supported a renewal of the Jacobite claim to the throne for Charles Edward Stuart (Bonnie Prince Charlie) who arrived in Scotland in 1745. Popular in Scotland, there was little Jacobite support in England even from Catholics.

At the Battle of Culloden–the last battle on British soil–the Jacobites were

Above: George II, c. 1727. *The Art Archive/ Handel Museum Halle/Alfredo Dagli Orti AA356273*

obliterated by the British Government Army. Finally, in 1748, the War of the Austrian Succession concluded in peace with Maria Theresa becoming Archduchess of Austria.

The Prince of Wales died suddenly in 1751 and his son Prince George soon received his title. In 1752 Britain changed from the Julian Calendar to the Gregorian Calendar and in the process lost eleven days (between September 2 and 14), an event many of the peasantry found deeply disturbing.

In October 1760 King George II died suddenly aged 76 from a ruptured aneurysm. He was buried in Westminster Abbey.

Above: George II commemorative identifying his birth and regnal dates; obverse shows a portrait of him in old age.
via Jo St. Mart

Right: George II in his garter robes.
Bridgeman Art Library/Getty Images 71901932

George III
House of Hanover
1738–1820 (r. 1760–1820)

The first Hanoverian king to be born in London and to speak English as his native tongue, George William Frederick was the eldest son of Frederick, Prince of Wales, and Augusta of Saxe-Gotha. He became heir apparent in 1751 when his father died, and Prince of Wales soon after. In October 1760 his grandfather, George II, died and he succeeded to general acclaim as George III. He had a long and eventful reign but his first priority was to find a queen: he married Duchess Sophia Charlotte of Mecklenburg-Strelitz in September 1761 and both were crowned at Westminster Abbey a fortnight later. Over time they had nine sons and six daughters. Unlike the rest of his family, George never took a mistress, a fact which made him much admired and liked by his subjects.

Politically George favored the Tories, leading the Whigs to criticize him. The American colonies were becoming more expensive to protect and more difficult to govern. In the Royal

Far left: At the Battle of Dettingen, June 27, 1743, George II became the last British king to lead his troops into battle. *Bridgeman Art Library/Getty Images 57297566*

Left: George III in the robes of the Order of the Garter. *The Art Archive AA401927*

Proclamation of 1763 to limit the cost of frontier warfare George announced a limit to the westward expansion of the American colonies–this was intended to compel colonists to negotiate with Native Americans. Irrelevant to most settlers, the Proclamation Line nevertheless was a grievance for a few vocal expansionists. In 1770 most custom duties except tea tax were withdrawn: the protest was the Boston Tea Party and the situation worsened until armed conflict broke out in April 1775–the American Revolution. Current opinion is that George III had little to do with causing the problems, rather it was his politicians. Soon Britain was also at war with France and then Spain, who together planned an armada to invade Britain and conquer London.

In 1781 George III offered to abdicate as the war in the colonies got worse; he was refused and finally conceded defeat and agreed to peace negotiations. The Treaty of Paris (1783) formally ended the American Revolutionary War with Britain recognizing the independence of the 13 American states; in the Treaties of Versailles (1783), Britain gave up Florida to Spain.

Meanwhile back in Parliament the Whigs and Tories were continually fighting for power and George had to

Left: George III. In 1783 the American Revolutionary War ended with Britain granting independence to the 13 American colonies. *Library of Congress, Prints & Photographs LC-USZ62-7819*

work with whoever had the majority whether he liked them or not. Finally, his preference, headed by William Pitt the Younger, won a Parliamentary majority and king and prime minister were able to work in harmony. To the annoyance of his advisors, George conscientiously read all his government papers and liked to voice his opinion on a wide variety of topics, and would use his influence when he felt moved to.

In summer 1788 George's mental health collapsed: modern science indicates that he suffered from porphyria, an inherited chemical disorder which affects the nervous system. His episodes of serious dementia caused parliament to debate the provisions for a regency. Prince Frederick, Duke of York was about to be authorized to become regent when the king recovered and resumed control of government. Throughout his father's reign the Prince Frederick was the target of robust criticism for his extravagant and flamboyant lifestyle and his numerous indiscretions, including his mistresses.

Across the English Channel in 1789 the French Revolution started and the British nobility were worried. Four years later France declared war on Great Britain meaning armies had to be gathered and taxes raised to pay for

Right: George III in his coronation robes, 1762. *via Jo St. Mart*

them. In May 1800 James Hadfield, a religious fanatic, tried to assassinate the king when he fired a pistol at him at the Theatre Royal, Drury Lane.

On January 1, 1801, the United Kingdom of Great Britain and Ireland came into being following the Act of Union in 1800; at the same time George dropped the long-standing British claim to the throne of France. In 1801 Britain and France made peace but war broke out again within months, and a Napoleonic invasion of England became a real threat. All over the country volunteers joined the armed forces to fight the invader–but following Admiral Lord Nelson's comprehensive victory at the Battle of Trafalgar the threat of invasion ended.

By 1810 the king's health was deteriorating. He was near blind and in constant pain from rheumatism as well as suffering great distress when his youngest daughter Princess Amelia died. The Regency Act 1811 made the Prince of Wales regent for the remainder of his reign. Later that year George III become completely insane, never to recover. He lived away from the public gaze at Windsor until his death. In his absence Britain was victorious in the Napoleonic wars and Hanover became a kingdom instead of an electorate: George III became king of Hanover. Oblivious to everything, he became increasingly deaf and did not know when his wife died in 1818, nor when his son the Duke of Kent died a few days before him. Poor old George III finally passed away aged 81 on January 29, 1820 at Windsor Castle where he was buried.

George IV
House of Hanover
1762–1830 (r. 1820–1830)

George Augustus Frederick was born at St. James's Palace the second son of George III and Queen Charlotte. Well educated and intelligent, George never got on with his father the king, much of the conflict was over his extravagant lifestyle and flamboyant behavior, his radicalism, and Whig political leanings.

In 1783, just after turning 21, George fell deeply in love with the twice widowed, Roman Catholic Maria Fitzherbert. Forbidden to marry her without the king's consent (which he knew he would never get), they married in December 1785 and both pledged to keep their union secret; the marriage was not legally valid as it violated the Royal Marriage Act of 1772.

The prince's high living escalated his debts until in 1787 his allies in parliament proposed a parliamentary grant for him to alleviate his debts; confirming rumors about his marriage would have scuppered the grant so it was roundly denied. The grant was awarded: £161,000 for debts and £60,000 for improvements to his official residence Carlton House.

During summer 1788 George III's mental condition was sufficiently bad for parliament to consider a regency: after much argument and just as it was

Above: The Duke of Wellington describing the field of Waterloo to King George IV. *Bridgeman Art Library/Getty Images 57557429*

Left: While Prince Regent, George enjoyed an extravagant and scandalous lifestyle before taking the throne as George IV. *The Art Archive/ National Gallery of Ireland Dublin AA347090*

agreed that the prince would take over, George recovered his wits. However the prince's debts were still mounting and the king refused to help him financially unless he married his first cousin, Caroline of Brunswick: they were married in April 1795. The marriage was a disaster and they formally separated after the birth of Princess Charlotte in 1796, with the Prince of Wales returning to the arms of Mrs. Fitzherbert, and Caroline moving to Europe where she also took lovers. Additionally the prince had a number of mistresses and a couple of illegitimate children.

By 1795 the Prince of Wales had debts of £630,000, Parliament came to his aid and granted him an annual sum of £65,000, then a further £60,000 in 1803 until in 1806 his original debt was finally cleared–then only the new debts accrued after 1795 remained.

In 1810 the king again succumbed to madness and this time the Prince of Wales became regent on January 5, 1811, for the next nine years. The burning topic of debate was whether or not to legislate for Catholic emancipation. On May 10, 1812, Prime Minister Spencer Perceval was assassinated by a lunatic, but the status quo was quickly reestablished with his Tory party eager to prosecute the war in Europe against Napoleon.

George III died in 1820 and the Prince Regent became George IV: he had grown obese thanks to his luxurious lifestyle and was allegedly addicted to laudanum, an alcoholic preparation of opium. He refused to allow his estranged wife Caroline to be recognized as queen and he attempted to get a divorce, but was dissuaded when he realized all his dirty washing would be made public and Caroline was very popular with the people. George was crowned in a lavish ceremony at Westminster Abbey on July 19, 1821, and Caroline was turned away at the door: she fell violently ill the same evening and died aged 53 three weeks later. She maintained that she had been poisoned; her doctors thought it was a blockage in her intestine.

Huge and largely immobile and ridiculed by his subjects, George IV spent most of his time at Windsor Castle but intervened to stop Catholic emancipation, a reversal of his previous stance. However, after bitter disagreements the Catholic Relief Act was given royal assent in April 1829.

On June 26, 1830 George IV died aged 67 at Windsor Castle and was buried there. Cause of death was obesity and associated ailments. He was not greatly mourned. His only child, Charlotte had died in 1817 so the crown passed to his brother William.

Left: The Prince of Wales was constantly lampooned in the press for his greed. *The Art Archive/British Museum/Eileen Tweedy AA347033*

Right: George IV as he preferred to be seen. *via Jo St. Mart*

William IV
House of Hanover
1765–1837 (r. 1830–1837)

William was the third son of George III and Queen Charlotte and was born at Buckingham House, London. Not expected to inherit the throne, he was sent aged 13 to join the Royal Navy as a midshipman. He was at the Battle of Cape St. Vincent and served in New York during the American War of Independence. By 1789 he had become a Rear Admiral and commander of HMS Valiant. His father made him the Duke of Clarence and Earl of Munster in 1790, and he left the navy. When war against France was declared in 1793 William expected but was not given a command, even in 1811 when he was made Admiral of the Fleet, he still saw no action.

In 1791 William set up his household with Dorothea Bland, an Irish actress known by her stage name as Mrs Jordan; together they had five sons and five daughters all of whom were given the surname FitzClarence. In 1811 the couple parted after 20 years together, their debts had driven them apart.

To stem his debts William needed a wealthy wife but there was little suitablke

Above: Statue of William IV. *Westminster Council/Jo St. Mart*

Above left: William IV, the "Sailor King." *Hulton Archive/Getty Images 3062558*

Right: William IV in formal robes. *The Art Archive/Musée du Château de Versailles/Gianni Dagli Orti AA363354*

choice other than 25-year-old Princess Adelaide of Saxe-Meiningen–he was 27 years older. They married in July 1818 and the marriage proved happy, although none of their children survived infancy. In 1820 the Prince Regent became King George IV, with his brother, Prince Frederick, Duke of York, next in line, and then his other brother William to follow. However, when the Duke of York died childless in 1827, William was left heir presumptive at over 60 years old.

George IV died in June 1830 and William inherited the throne at the age of 64. For his time in the Royal Navy he was nicknamed the Sailor King. He was crowned in September 1831 and took his responsibilities seriously and attended his state business with interest. His reign was dominated by the Reform crisis when the Whigs (with popular public support) tried to make the House of Commons more representative of the people and not just the prerogative of the aristocracy. Despite William's support two reform bill failed because of Tory opposition, and countrywide demonstrations for reform threatened to become openly violent. With civil violence a real possibility the Reform Act 1832 was finally passed.

William died of heart failure following illness at Windsor Castle in June 1837; he was 71. Without children his heir was his niece Princess Victoria of Kent, who had only come of age a month earlier, but under Salic Law a woman could not rule in Hanover so that inheritance went to his brother Ernest, Duke of Cumberland. Earnest, in turn, was heir presumptive of the United Kingdom until Victoria had her first child in 1840.

Victoria
House of Hanover
1819–1901 (r. 1837–1901)

Alexandrina Victoria was the only child of Edward, Duke of Kent, and Princess Victoria of Saxe-Coburg-Saalfeld, and when she was born at Kensington Palace she was fifth in line to the throne after her father and three middle-aged uncles, all of whom were unlikely to produce legitimate male heirs. Her father died eight months later in January 1820 aged 53 leaving Victoria heir apparent; with this position in mind she was carefully schooled in a variety of subjects. Her first language was German and only after the age of three learned English and French.

Victoria was just 18 when her uncle William IV died–his publicly stated ambition was to live long enough to prevent her mother the Duchess of Kent becoming regent. She became queen on June 20, 1837, and was crowned on June 28, 1838.

Inevitably Victoria was the most eligable young woman in Europe and had many suitors: her uncle William IV favored Prince Alexander of the

Right: Statues of Queen Victoria were placed across the British Empire. *Westminster Council/Jo St. Mart*

Far right: The young Queen Victoria in her robes of state. *The Art Archive AA401632*

Netherlands but her other uncle King
Leopold I of Belgium favored his
nephew, Prince Albert of Saxe-Coburg
Gotha–he was also Victoria's first cousin
as he was her mother's brother's son–
and arranged for them to meet in 1836,
Victoria was quickly smitten and
proposed to him in 1839. Just before
their marriage Albert was naturalized
and granted an annuity of £30,000 from
the queen, although parliament refused
to make him a peer, probably because of
anti-German feeling. They married in
February 1840 and went on to have nine
children between 1840 and 1857; in time
eight of their children married into
European royal families, earning her the
nickname "Grandmother of Europe."

Victoria's first government was led
by Lord Melbourne the leader of the
Whig party. She admired him
enormously and with his experience
and guidance started to learn the ropes
of power. Privately (via letters) her other
principal advisor was her mother's
brother, King Leopold I of Belgium.
However, after their marriage Albert
became Victoria's chief political advisor
and confidant, although rather to his
annoyance, his official title was HRH
The Prince Consort, not king. Their first
child, Victoria, was born in November
1840. The Regency Act 1840 was then
passed to make Albert regent should
Victoria die before the child reached her
majority.

The public as a whole were delighted to have a pretty young queen on
the throne after so many old men,
but even so, once in 1840 and twice in
1842 Victoria was the target of assassination attempts. In the later 1840s Victoria was furious that members of her

government, particularly Foreign Secretary, Lord Palmerston would take political decisions without consulting or informing her: Prime Minister, Lord John Russell, largely ignored her objections. Unlike her predecessors Victoria had to learn to be a constitutional monarch with considerable influence but few actual powers.

Through the early years the royal coffers were low, but thanks to Albert's careful and intelligent management by 1844 they had sufficient funds to buy Osborne House on the Isle of Wight and then Balmoral Castle in Scotland in 1852. 1848 was the year of European revolutions thanks to the general economic crisis and Albert in particular was worried for his relatives. There was no real taste for revolution in Britain as absolutist monarchy had long been eliminated in favor of a constitutional monarch ruling through an elected government. Even so, in 1849 and 1850 Victoria survived two further attacks on her person, both assailants were sentenced to seven years penal transportation.

Albert's role as Royal Consort gave him great influence which he used to improve social conditions, education, and the arts and sciences generally. Perhaps his greatest triumph was the Great Exhibition of 1851 in Hyde Park, which through Albert's patronage and determination—against vocal opposition—was a

Left: Stained glass window of Victoria in Christ Church, Oxford. A popular monarch, her image was found everywhere. *History Department UCL via Jo St. Mart*

great popular success. The Exhibition opened in May 1851 to great acclaim and from the huge profits land was bought in South Kensington for educational and cultural institutions, one of which later became the Victoria and Albert Museum. Albert also campaigned to modernize the army but was opposed by Lord Palmerston, although in 1854 as the Crimean War unfolded, his case was proven.

In March 1861, Victoria's mother, the Duchess of Kent, died leaving her daughter distraught, so Albert took on many of her duties although he was suffering at the time from chronic stomach troubles. Within a few months, on December 14, 1861, Albert died of typhoid fever aged 42 at Windsor Castle. Initially unpopular with the British public, he had earned their respect through his faithful support of the queen and his sensible advice to her. Queen Victoria was inconsolable and wore mourning black for the rest of her life. Victoria felt much of the blame for Albert's death was the fault of Edward, Prince of Wales, whose scandalous liason with an Irish actress had caused an already sick Albert to travel to Cambridge University to take him to task.

Left: Victoria in her coronation robes, 1837. *The Art Archive/Alfredo Dagli Orti AA348681*

Right: A young Queen Victoria dressed for the theater. In her youth she was noted for her gaity and outgoing nature. *The Art Archive/ Eileen Tweedy AA348642*

Left: Bronze statue of Queen Victoria at Queen's Cross, Aberdeen, depicted in her more familiar stocky old age. *Fotolia/Vim Woodenhands*

Victoria withdrew from public life choosing to live privately at Windsor, Balmoral, or Osborne House on the Isle of Wight: she became known as the "Widow of Windsor." At first her subjects supported her but after a few years people started to complain at her self-indulgence and apparent lack of interest in the state of the nation and republican rumblings were heard. She did not neglect her official duties with her ministers and foreign visitors but avoided public appearances until coaxed out of seclusion by her prime minister, Benjamin Disraeli. By the 1880s Victoria's popularity had recovered and in 1887 Victoria celebrated her golden jubilee (50 years on the throne), and then her Diamond Jubilee in 1897.

Throughout her reign British explorers, colonists, and empire builders had spread her dominions far and wide. The British Empire was the great superpower of the century–it was said that she ruled an empire on which the sun never set–and Queen Victoria its much loved and revered sovereign.

On January 22, 1901, at Osbourne House, Queen Victoria died at the age of 81 of a cerebral hemorrhage. She was placed in her coffin wearing a white dress and a wedding veil and buried beside Albert in the family mausoleum at Windsor. She had reigned for over 63 years, the first of the modern constitutional monarchs.

Edward VII

**House of Saxe Coburg-Gotha
1841–1910 (r. 1901–1910)**

Albert Edward was born at Buckingham Palace in November 1841, the first son of Queen Victoria and Albert, the Prince Consort. From the age of seven, Bertie as he was called, was rigorously educated as befitted a constitutional monarch; however, he was noted to be full of natural charm rather than any great intellect. From inclination he would have joined the military but was excluded because of his position as heir apparent.

Edward soon gained a reputation as a playboy, a course of action he decided on when informed that he was to marry Princess Alexandra of Denmark. While watching military maneuvers in Ireland he started a liaison with an Irish actress: when Albert and Victoria heard of the scandal, the former although ill, went to

Above: John Bull says, "Yes it's yours, Albert, but you'll have to wait until next Thursday before you get it." Edward VII was lampooned for the postponement of his coronation because of illness. *The Art Archive/Culver Pictures AA407102*

Cambridge to reprimand him. Two weeks later Albert died of typhoid, and Victoria never forgave Edward for she thought the visit had caused Albert's death.

After a tour of the Middle East Edward returned to England to marry Alexandra at Windsor in March 1863. Together they led a sociable and lavish lifestyle in London and at Sandringham House in Norfolk: Queen Victoria greatly disapproved. They had six children, one of whom died in infancy, and the eldest Albert Victor died of pneumonia in 1892. Additionally Edward had numerous mistresses, most notably the popular actress Lily Langtry and the society beauty Alice Keppel. Edward's infidelity was apparently accepted by Alexandria but his mother and society as a whole were generally scaldalized.

When Queen Victoria withdrew into widowhood Edward became her representative at public ceremonies and official functions, but Victoria would not make him her official deputy until a few years before her death in 1898, instead he became a popular leader of London society and fashionable life. Politically they held opposite opinions–Victoria supported Germany while Bertie supported Denmark, particularly pertinent

Left: Edward VII in the uniform of Colonel of the 10th Hussars. *The Art Archive/Eileen Tweedy AA346873*

Right: Edward VII in the uniform of the Hungarian 12th Hussar Regiment, presented to him by the Austrian Emperor Franz Josef. *The Art Archive/Museum der Stadt Wien AA332202*

during the Schleswig-Holstein Question in 1864. Between his mother and his father-in-law Edward was related to almost every royal house in Europe.

In winter 1871 Bertie caught typhoid: the public and his mother were hugely concerned and greatly relieved by his recovery–his popularity with both improved enormously. In 1875 Edward journeyed to India for eight months. The tour was a great success not least because Edward treated everyone with equal courtesy and enthusiasm.

Queen Victoria died on January 22, 1901, when Edward was 59. He chose to rule as Edward VII rather than Albert as his mother had wanted. Edward and Alexandra were crowned at Westminster Abbey in August 1902. Edward continued to vacation abroad and was instrumental in ending the centuries-old hostility and suspicion between England and France. He also became the first British monarch to visit Russia in 1908.

Excluded from British politics in which he had liberal leanings, Edward used his influence to reform the army and modernize of the Home Fleet.

Edward had always been a heavy smoker and in March 1910 when he was staying in Biarritz, in southwestern France he collapsed with bronchitis. A few weeks later he was able to return to Buckingham Palace–he had been criticized for staying away during a political crisis but his illness was unknown to the public–and almost immediately suffered several heart attacks and died.

Left: Edward VII after his coronation in 1902. *Wikipedia via Jo St. Mart*

George V
House of Windsor
1865–1936 (r. 1910–1936)

Born when his father, Albert Edward, and mother, Alexandra, were Prince and Princess of Wales in 1865 at Marlborough House in London, as the second son George was not expected to succeed to the throne,. Being only 15 months younger, he and Albert were educated together. In 1877 both brothers were sent to Dartmouth for three years' naval training, in the course of which they traveled the world: George even got tattooed in Japan with a dragon on his arm. On their return Albert was sent to Cambridge but George was allowed to remain with the navy.

In 1891 Albert became engaged to his second cousin Princess Victoria Mary of Teck (known as May), but within six weeks he died of pneumonia: George became second in line to the throne and had to leave the navy to start learning his new political role. Queen Victoria still wanted the princess in the family and instructed George to propose: she also made him the Duke of York. George and Mary married in July 1893 in London, then spent much of their time on the Sandringham estate where George enjoyed shooting and stamp collecting. Together they had five sons and a daughter.

When George's father Edward VII became king, he and his wife assumed a greater public role. In 1901 they toured

Right: Early photograph of George V. *The Art Archive/Private Collection MD AA397322*

the empire and in November George was made Prince of Wales and included in state matters by his father. In 1906 George toured India where he was thrilled by the country but disgusted by the racism and openly insisted on greater Indian involvement in their own country's government.

In May 1910 Edward VII died and George became George V; he and Queen Mary were crowned at Westminster Abbey in June 1911. Their first official visit was a grand tour of India later that same year.

Between 1914 and 1918 Britain and Germany were opposed in the First World War. Throughout the conflict the king visited servicemen at the front line and in hospital and agitated for civil treatment for German prisoners of war and conscientious objectors. King Edward and Kaiser Wilhelm II were first cousins and the entire British royal family had German ancestors and titles, a fact which caused great unease with the British public. Accordingly, in July 1917 George changed his family name from the House of Saxe-Coburg-Gotha to the House of Windsor and gave up all his German titles. To many of his relatives who also lost their titles he gave British peerages and names.

Meanwhile the 1916 Easter Rising in Dublin resulted in the creation of the Irish Free State, while the six northern counties remained British.

Right: Two of Victoria's grandsons, George V (right) and Kaiser Wilhelm II of Germany, in Berlin after the wedding of the Kaiser's daughter, June 6, 1913. *The Art Archive/Culver Pictures AA407120*

Above: George V in full uniform. *Library of Congress Prints & Photographs Division LC-DIG-ggbain-04883*

Right : George V photographed in 1914. *The Art Archive/Bibliothèque des Arts Décoratifs Paris /Gianni Dagli Orti AA419942*

King George's relationship with his son and heir Prince Edward deteriorated with time as he despaired of Edward's loose living and penchant for other men's wives. He dreaded how he would behave when he became king. Instead he greatly preferred his second son Prince Albert (later George VI).

In 1935 George V celebrated his silver jubilee but by 1938 his lifelong heavy smoking resulted in a variety of serious breathing problems including emphysema and pleurisy, so he allowed Edward to take over many of his official duties while he retired for sea air to Bognor Regis in Sussex. In January 1936 he died near midnight at Sandringham House. He was buried at Windsor.

Left: Woodrow Wilson, 28th U.S. President (left), with King George V, in London, December 1918. *The Art Archive/ Culver Pictures AA402702*

Edward VIII
House of Windsor
1894–1972 (r. January–December 1936)

The first son of the Duke of York (later George VI) and Mary of Teck was born in Richmond, London at the close of the 19th century. Edward became Prince of Wales in June 1910 a month after his father became king. In 1911 he joined the Royal Navy; then, during the First World War served with the Grenadier Guards but was kept away from the fighting. However he did make frequent visits which made him popular with the soldiers. In 1918 he went up in his first military flight and later became a pilot.

As Prince of Wales Edward represented the king both at home and abroad–between 1919 and 1935 he made 16 tours to various outposts of empire. In the 1920s he was the most eligible bachelor in the world and the center of much attention and gossip, especially his penchant for married women, the most notorious of which was the twice married and twice divorced Wallis Simpson. The king greatly disapproved of the relationship

Far left: Edward, Prince of Wales left, with his brother George, Duke of Kent at the opening of the International Peace Bridge, Niagara Falls, June 1, 1927. *The Art Archive/Culver Pictures AA407863*

Left: Edward, Prince of Wales in naval uniform, c.1913. *The Art Archive/Culver Pictures AA407865*

and the personal relationship with his son became very difficult.

On January 20, 1936, King George V died and Edward became king. His government was anxious about the king with regards to Mrs. Simpson and their belief that he would interfere with government. Moreover, it was becoming clear that Edward planned to marry Mrs. Simpson and plans for a secular coronation (because she was a divorcée) were drawn up using the Banqueting House in Whitehall instead of Westminster Abbey. On November 16, 1936, Edward summoned his prime minister Stanley Baldwin and announced his intention to marry. Baldwin told him it was unacceptable to his subjects and in the laws of the Church of England. Edward proposed a compromise: Wallis would not become queen and any children would not inherit; the British parliament refused– as did almost all the parliaments of the Dominions (under law their permission was needed too).

Edward announced if he did not get his way he would abdicate: Baldwin replied with three choices: give up Mrs. Simpson; abdicate and marry her; marry her, causing the government to resign and create a constitutional crisis. Forced into a corner, on December 10, 1936, Edward signed the Instrument of Abdication in front of his three brothers. The following night he broadcast to a shocked nation and empire explaining how he would not give up the woman he loved. He then left the country.

Prince Albert, Duke of York, became king and Edward was given the title Duke of Windsor. In June 1937 the Duke of Windsor and Wallis Simpson married

Above: Statue of Edward, Prince of Wales in Aberystwyth, Wales. It is probably the only public statue of him anywhere. *via Jo St. Mart*

Right: Formal photographic portrait of George VI. As the second son he had not expected to become king. *via Jo St. Mart*

in France, King George VI forbade all members of the royal family to attend the ceremony. Edward was allowed an allowance (not as much as he wanted) on condition he did not return to Britain without invitation, but Wallis was not given the title Her Royal Highness (HRH) as he constantly demanded. They had no children.

In 1937 the Duke and Duchess of Windsor visited Hitler in German and were suspected of being Nazi appeasers and sympathizers, making them even more personally unpopular in Britain. During World War II the duke was appointed Governor of the Bahamas; speculation still continues that Hitler planned to reinstate the duke as king when he invaded Britain. After the war the duke and duchess moved to France where they remained for the rest of their lives. The duke died in May 1972 of throat cancer (he was a heavy smoker) and after lying in state he was buried at Windsor. The duchess died in 1986 and was buried beside him.

George VI
House of Windsor
1895–1952 (r. 1936–1952)

Prince Albert, Bertie to his family, was born on the Sandringham Estate, the son of the Duke and Duchess of York and great grandson of Queen Victoria, on the anniversary of his great grandfather Albert's death. As the second son and fourth in line to the throne he was not expected to inherit the crown. He was not a strong child and suffered from a stammer, chronic

Above: The Duke and Duchess of York, before they became George VI and Queen Elizabeth. *The Art Archive/Private Collection MD AA397323*

to the throne when his father became King George V.

During World War I Albert saw action as a midshipman at the Battle of Jutland (1916) but then a duodenal ulcer stopped further service. In 1918 he was sent to the naval training establishment at Cranwell which within the year became the Royal Air Force and Albert transferred across the services. In the 1920s he started to help his father out with royal duties visiting factories, railyards, and mines and earning himself the nickname the "Industrial Prince."

In 1920 Albert met and fell in love with a commoner, Lady Elizabeth Bowes-Lyon, daughter of the Earl of Strathmore and Kinghorne, they married in April 1923 in Westminster Abbey. They had two daughters, Elizabeth and Margaret, and lived quietly in London. In January 1936 King George V died and the Prince of Wales became Edward VIII and Albert heir presumptive. Within a year the abdication crisis had forced the uncrowned Edward VIII from the throne and installed a very reluctant Albert (three days off his 41st birthday): he chose to reign as King George VI.

Coping with the aftermath of the abdication was his first job: he conferred the title Duke of Windsor to his demoted brother and had to buy his private estates of Sandringham House and Balmoral Castle from him. George VI was crowned on May 12, 1937 (the date initially intended for Edward). It was a tense time with war in Europe becoming more inevitable by the day. In 1939 the king and queen toured Canada—as king and queen of Canada—

stomach problems, and knock knees, all of which made him very withdrawn. Age 14 he became a naval cadet at the Royal Naval College on the Isle of Wight and then at Dartmouth in Devon. Then in May 1910 he became second in line

and briefly visited the U.S.–in a political move to familiarize and popularize Britain with the North American public at a time when war was about to erupt in Europe.

War was declared in 1939 and the king and queen announced they would stay in London and not move to Canada and safety as had been suggested. They repeatedly made morale-boosting visits to factories, bombed areas, particularly the devastated East End of London, and abided by the public food rationing their subjects had no choice but to observe. Their personal popularity and that of their two girls soared. In 1939 George went to France to visit the British Expeditionary Force, in 1943 to North Africa after the victory at El Alamein, in 1944 to the Normandy beaches 10 days after D-Day, then later Italy and the Netherlands.

The period after the war saw the dissolution of the British Empire (it had started with the Balfour declaration in 1926) and the emergence of the

Above: George VI, General Mark Clark, and General Sir Harold Alexander, in a command car before leaving to review Fifth Army troops. *The Art Archive/National Archives Washington DC AA399225*

Left: Princess Elizabeth before she became queen; she was raised to be the monarch from a very early age. *The Art Archive AA527385*

Commonwealth of Nations. Never a strong man physically, the stress of the war coupled with his heavy smoking took a toll on George's health. He developed lung cancer and in September 1951 had his left lung and its accompanying tumor removed. On February 6, 1952 he died in his sleep from a coronary thrombosis at Sandringham, at the age of 56. Princess Elizabeth, was in Kenya on tour, she flew back immediately. After lying in state at Westminster Hall George VI was buried in Windsor.

Elizabeth II
House of Windsor
1926–present (r. 1952–present)

Born in Mayfair, London to Albert and Elizabeth, the Duke and Duchess of York, Elizabeth Alexandra Mary, third in line to the throne, was not expected to succeed to the crown until her uncle the Prince of Wales (later King Edward VIII) unexpectedly abdicated in December 1936. Also, had her parents had a son, he would have taken precedence. Her father became King George VI in 1936 and their quiet family life completely changed.

Age 13 at the start of World War II, Elizabeth and her sister Margaret (born 1930) were evacuated to Windsor Castle, close to but not actually in London. Her father the king carefully protected her from entering public life too young despite various suggestions and requests for her to do so from his politicians. In 1944 Elizabeth was appointed a Counsellor of State and in her father's absence in Italy carried out some official business of state for the first time. Elizabeth first started royal duties on her own in 1945 when she accompanied her parents to meet Commonwealth service personnel. Later that year and to show solidarity with the British people in wartime, she joined the Women's Auxiliary Territorial Service where she trained as a driver and then served as a military truck driver; by war's end she was a Junior Commander.

In November 1947 Elizabeth married her second cousin once removed, Philip Mountbatten, Duke of Edinburgh, (formerly Prince Philippos of Greece and Denmark). He was still a serving officer in the Royal Navy and between 1949 and 1951 they lived in Malta while Philip served there. The first of their four children and the heir presumptive, Charles, was born in 1948.

By 1951 King George VI's health was noticeably deteriorating and Elizabeth took over some of his public duties which included a number of foreign visits. In January 1952 Elizabeth and the Duke set out for a tour of Australia and New Zealand, a trip originally planned for her parents; they were in Kenya when news of the king's death arrived on February 6. The trip was cancelled and the couple returned to Britain. Elizabeth was crowned on June 2 at Westminster Abbey, for the first time the ceremony was televised and seen by an estimated 20 million people.

Right: Queen Elizabeth II photographed in 2007. *via Jo St. Mart*

The British Empire had started to be legally dismantled in 1931 to become the Commonwealth of Nations and this process continued under Elizabeth. In 1953–54 Elizabeth and Prince Philip circumnavigated the globe on a six-month tour meeting heads of state and religious leaders around the world. This pattern of important public foreign tours continued at regular interval sthroughout her reign, although it decreased somewhat in her later years; in 1965 she became the first British monarch in 52 years to visit Germany, the land of many of her ancestors, and in 1991 she became the first British monarch to address a joint session of the U.S. Congress.

In 1977 Elizabeth celebrated her Silver Jubilee as monarch with a nationwide tour and many Common-wealth visits, racking up a total of 56,000 miles; in 2002 she celebrated her Golden Jubilee with further tours of the nation and Commonwealth. She is currently the oldest reigning monarch in British history and only Victoria sat on the throne for longer. As a constitutional monarch the queen is officially impartial and has no power over government; she does have influence through her weekly private audiences with her prime minister. Throughout her reign Elizabeth has read through volumes of state papers, making her better informed and more experienced than any politician.

Right: Smiling in the summer sunshine, Elizabeth II steps out of St. Paul's Cathedral, London, following a service to celebrate her 80th birthday on April 21, 2006. *Jo St. Mart*

Scottish Monarchy

As with England, Scotland's monarchy has its roots in the period after the Romans retreated from the British Isles in the fifth century. Unlike England, Scotland was never subdued by the Romans, although their influence over the period was considerable. Regular invasions; the controlling factors of the wall and its garrisons; trade–all these things meant that the lowlands of Scotland were greatly affected by the Romans' presence.

The name Scotland itself is indicative of Roman involvement: the Scoti was what the Romans called the Gaelic-speaking Celts in Ireland who raided and settled the western areas of Scotland. It was the people the Romans called the Picts that formed their main enemy. It is possible that it was a Gael from the western isles–the mythhic Cinead mac Ailpin (Kenneth MacAlpin)–who joined the kingdoms of Scots and Picts, but there is no straightforward account of the period and much historical disputation. Nevertheless, Kenneth MacAlpin is recognized by tradition as first in the line of what would become Scotland's monarchy in 843.

Geography plays a huge part in Scottish history, in particular the divide between the Highland and Lowland Scots. The Romans sought–as they did everywhere–to play on political divisions within the tribes around the wall promoting a north-south divide that has been ever-present in Scottish history. Moreover, the early history of Scotland was not just influenced by those south of Hadrian's Wall. Most of the northern and western isles–and, indeed, parts of the northern mainland– came under Viking, particularly Norwegian, domination from the ninth century. This includes those areas that had been settled by the Scots from Ireland. Norwegian rule would continue in the islands into the thirteenth century and Scottish monarchs would not gain full control of this area until well into the fifteenth century.

The first King of the Picts (Rex Pictorum) may have been a figment of medieval myth, but by 889 his grandson–Donald II–was fighting against Viking invaders of what the Gaelic rulers called the Kingdom of Alba. The battles against the Vikings continued into the tenth century and led to an alliance in 945 between Malcolm I and Edmund of England: a rare example of good relations between the two countries!

In the aftermath of the Norman invasion and subjection of England, Scotland itself was closely linked to England. Indeed, this period is known as the Scoto-Norman period and the monarchs and many of the nobility

spoke French. This was promoted by the fact that a number of Scottish monarchs in this period spent many years living in the English court–particularly Malcolm III in the court of the pro-Norman Edward the Confessor (Malcolm married Margaret of Wessex); Duncan II who spent twenty years a hostage in the court of William I of England; and also David I. As an example of the proximity of the courts, Alexander I fought in Wales alongside Henry I and Malcolm IV was

concessions from the Scots, choosing John Balliol as king–but getting him to swear fealty to the English crown before he acceded in 1292. This was a state of affairs that could not continue for long and, sure enough, Edward undermined and humiliated Balliol to such an extent that the Scottish parliament appointed the Council of Twelve to rule in Balliol's name, and allied with France.

The Scottish "Wars of Independence" that ensued were bloody and ensured a legacy of enmity between the two countries. The death of Edward I, a massive defeat of the English at Bannockburn, and the emergence of Robert Bruce as leader–after he had murdered the opposition–saw a new dynasty of Scottish monarchs. Edward III, would get embroiled in wars in France. To keep his back safe, Edward signed the Treaty of Northampton, recognizing Scotland's independence and marrying his sister Joan to the Bruce's son, David II.

The peace did not last and soon David II was languishing in an English jail. His death, childless, in 1371 saw another new dynasty with the accession of the first Stewart monarch: 230 years later his descendant, James VI became King James I of England.

And that was that. In 1707 the Acts of Union took effect, thus joining the two countries officially under one monarch. Bar Jacobite rebellions in 1715 and 1745, the latter ending in the bloodbath of Culloden that saw clan fighting clan, the two monarchies have stayed as one ever since.

knighted by Henry II after the siege of Toulouse in 1159. William I of Scotland fought against Henry II in the revolt of Henry's sons of 1173–1174 and ended up captured, ransomed, and having to swear fealty to the English king.

During this Scoto-Norman period the Scottish crown consolidated its position over the rest of Scotland eventually throwing out the Norwegians: the Treaty of Perth in 1266 ceded the Western Isles and the Isle of Man to Scotland. However, diplomacy kept the two countries linked. In 1286, when King Alexander III died, his heir was three-year old Margaret "the Maid of Norway"–the daughter of Eric II of Norway and Alexander's daughter Margaret. Unfortunately, she died in Orkney on the way to Scotland before her coronation.

Who was to succeed? Scotland's "Great Cause" was given to Edward I of England to arbitrate. Edward wrung

Left: The saltire of St. Andrew became the official flag of Scotland in 1606.

Cináed mac Ailpín
(Kenneth I MacAlpin)
House of Alpin
c. 810–858 (r. 843–858)

The Pictish king Cináed mac Ailpín is a king of myth as much as known fact. Even his ancestry is disputed: he might have been a Gael or a Pict. He was the son, it seems, of King Alpin II of Dál Riata (roughly present-day Argyll) and became king on his father's death in 839.

Cináed rose to power following a great battle against the Vikings in 839, when the Pictish King Uen and almost all his relatives and nobles died leaving a power vacuum–there were at least four contenders for the crown from the surviving members of the royal house. The initial victor was Drust X, but then Cináed defeated the Picts in battle in 841. Legend then says they got together at Scone where they all got drunk before Cináed and his Scots turned on the Picts and killed them eliminating all other contenders for the crown. Cináed was crowned King of the Picts and Scots in 843, the first king of the house of Alpin. His stronghold was at Fortevoit, near present-day Perth.

The 11th century Chronicle of the Kings of Alba (of which only one copy survives and resides in Paris, France) says Cináed was constantly under attack from the Vikings, and that he captured Melrose and burned Dunbar. In any event, the

Above: Scone Palace near Perth is the original home of the Stone of Destiny. *Scottish Tourist Board via Jo St. Mart*

remaining Picts wanted their throne back and continued fighting, but by 855 Cináed was firmly in control of all northern Scottish lands not held by the Vikings.

Thanks to the Viking raids and their extensive settlement across all the Scottish islands, mainland Scotland and Cináed's kingdom were almost completely cut off and isolated from Ireland, southern England, and Continental Europe. This had the result of strengthening the relationship between the Picts and the Gaels to eventually unite them as one people, the Alba.

In February 858 Cináed died from the effects of a tumor at the palace of Cinnbelachoir; he was buried on Iona. He left at least two sons and two daughters but was succeeded by his brother Domnall mac Ailpín (Donald I).

Left: Legend says that in A.D. 800 Kenneth MacAlpin was crowned the first king of Scotland here at Scone. *Scottish Tourist Board via Jo St. Mart*

Domnall mac Ailpín
(Donald mac Alpin)
House of Alpin
c. ?–862 (r. 858–862)

Domnall mac Ailpín was the younger son of King Alpin II of Dál Riata and brother of Cináed mac Ailpín (Kenneth I). Very little is known about him other than he was a "vigorous" soldier. During his short reign he consolidated his hold over the throne by suppressing all Pictish attempts to regain the crown. Additionally Domnall introduced the Laws of Aedh, which included the law of tanistry which essentially ensured that when the king died the next king would be elected, so the crown would pass to the most able member of the family—someone who had the strength and wisdom to protect the kingdom—and not to a young son unable to fight and rule. Over the following 150 or so years the law ensured that the crown alternated between the two increasingly distant lines of the House of Alpin, with the result of increasingly strained relations and the frequent murder of the crown's incumbent.

Domnall mac Ailpín died at at the palace of Cinnbelachoir in Perthshire in 862—the Chronicle of Melrose alone says he was assassinated—after reigning for four years and was buried on Iona. His elected successor was his nephew Constantine I, son of Cináed mac Ailpín.

Left: The Coronation throne encompasses the Stone of Destiny. *Library of Congress Prints and Photographs Division LC-DIG-ggbain-09425*

Caustantin mac Cináda
(Caustantín mac Cináeda)
House of Alpin
c. 836–877 (r. 863–877)

Elected king by the law of tanistry, Caustantín mac Cináeda was the son of Cináed mac Ailpín, and the nephew of his predecessor Domnall mac Ailpín. Throughout his reign Caustantín was fighting to consolidate and expand the Kingdom of Alba (Scotland); this was the period of great Viking raids yet Caustantín was a match for them in the mid-860s and defeated first Olaf the White (Amlaíb Conung) then Thorsten the Red in battle. His southern rival was Artgal, King of Strathclyde, who died in 872 (at the hands of the Vikings possibly when Caustantín refused to pay his ransom), and then placed his brother-in-law on the throne and in the process make Strathclyde a subordinate kingdom to Alba.

The Vikings returned in strength from Dublin and Yorkshire in 877 and landed in Fife where they established a settlement from where they could raid the eastern seaboard of Scotland. That same year Caustantín and his men met the Vikings at Inverdovat in northeast Fife, he was killed in battle and buried in Iona.

Left: The Dupplin Cross in Dunning church dates from c. 800 and shows an engraving of Constantine I. *Scottish Tourist Board via Jo St. Mart*

Domnall mac Caustantín (Donald II)

House of Alpin
c. 862–900 (r. 889–900)

Domnall mac Causantín was the son of Caustantín mac Cináeda (Constantine I). Overlooked for the crown when Eochaid and Giric took the throne, Domnall was later asked or perhaps ordered to kill Giric by Eochaid. Domnall duly despatched Giric at Dundurn near St. Fillans but returned to exile Eochaid to Gwynned in Wales.

Domnall took for himself the crowns of the Picts and Scots and of Strathclyde–and in the process becoming known as the King of Alba (instead of being the king of the Picts and Scots). He also became the first Scottish king to be recorded as fighting against the Highlanders. Domnall's contemporary was Sigurd the Mighty, the ravaging Viking who took for himself most of northern Scotland.

Domnall was killed by the Danes at the Battle of Dunnottar (900) near Montrose, and was buried on Iona.

Caustantín mac Aeda

(Constantine II)

House of Alpin
c. 874–952 (r. 900-943)

Causantín mac Aeda, son of King Aedh, succeeded as the king of the Picts and Scots on the death of his cousin Domnall mac Causantín. He too

Above: The cemetary surrounding Orans Chapel, Iona, is the burial place for generations of Scottish kings. *Scottish Tourist Board via Jo St. Mart*

inherited a land ravaged by the Vikings but in 904 at the Battle of Scone his victory drove the raiders out of mainland Scotland. Then, in the First and Second Battles of Corbridge in 914 and 918 he soundly defeated the Vikings who had settled in Northumberland.

With the threat of the Vikings diminished Causantín was able to turn his attention to governing his realm. He started the system of Mormaer in which sub-kings or earls were responsible for the protection and running of parts of his kingdom. Also Causantín ordered the church to become more Gaelic in character.

In 927 and then again in 934 Causantín submitted to King Athelstan of England to secure some kind of peace to the south. The Vikings had not gone away altogether, they still had considerable numbers in Dublin, so to improve the prospects of peace, in 937 Causantín married his daughter to Olaf III Guthfrithson, the Viking king in Dublin. Their combined army of Strathclyde Britons and Vikings invaded England in 937 and met the English army of King Athelstan at the Battle of Brunanburh where they were soundly defeated: one of Causantín's sons, Cellach was among the dead. As a result of the heavy defeat the Scots abandoned Lothian (including Edinburgh) to Northumbrian rule. Also, the battle is significant for establishing the approximate border between England and Scotland.

In 943 at the age of about 69, Causantín abdicated the throne after 43 years, so that Malcolm I could succeed him. Causantín withdrew to Culdee Monastery at St. Andrews, Fife where he became a monk. He died there in 952 and was probably buried there.

Máel Coluim mac Domnaill (Malcolm I)

House of Alpin
897–954 (r. 943–954)

Máel Coluim mac Domnaill was the son of Domnall mac Causantín, he was nicknamed "An Bodhbhdercc," meaning "Dangerous Red."

His intelligent leadership won him a reputation for wisdom and he became an ally of King Edmund I of England in their mutual fight against the scourge of the Viking raiders. In 945 Edmund had expelled Olaf Sihtricsson and his Vikings from Northumbria, devastated Cumbria (so the land would be of no use), and blinded the two sons of Domnall mac Causantín (Donald II) because a blind man could not be a warrior leader. To help keep the Vikings away, Edmund then allied himself with Máel and "let"

him the province of Strathclyde by way of reward. This alliance was probably renewed with King Edred, Edmund's successor to the English throne.

In 948 Eric Bloodaxe took York but was quickly driven out by Edred before Olaf Sihtricsson retook the city again in 949. Perhaps as part of the agreement Máel raided south against King Anlaf right across Northumbria as far as the River Tees taking many people and herds of cattle in the process. In 952 a battle was reported in the Ulster chronicle between the men of Alba, the Britons of Strathclyde, and the English against the Norsemen.

In 954 the men of Moray led by maormor (earl) Cellach revolted against Máel but were quickly surpressed and Cellach killed. However the problem was not thoroughly dealt with and one of Cellach's followers assassinated Máel at Auldearn. He was buried alongside his predecessors on Iona.

Donnchad mac Crínáin

(Duncan I)

House of Dunkeld
1001–1040 (r. 1034–1040)

Donnchad mac Crínáin succeeded to the throne without opposition because he was the grandson of Máel Coluim mac Cináeda, who had fathered no sons. Very little is known about Donnchad except that he appears as a greatly fictionalized figure in William Shakespear's Macbeth.

Donnchad married in 1030 but the chronicles disagree about his wife; she might have been called Suthen, or been

Above left: Reenactment of the Battle of Moray in 954 when the Earl of Cellach led a revolt against Malcolm I. *Scottish Tourist Board via Jo St. Mart*

Above: Malcolm I allied with the English against the Danish Vikings. *Getty Images via Jo St. Mart 51244225*

a cousin of Earl Siward Biornsson of Northumbria: however, in time two of their sons became kings. In 1039 Donnchad led his army into England where he besieged Durham, but they were soundly beaten. Donnchad managed to escape.

The following year Donnchad was challenged for the crown by Macbeth (Mac Bethad mac Findláich), who with his ally Earl Thorfinn of Orkney, made a bid for power. The three met in battle at Pitgaveny near Elgin in August 1040 and Donnchad was killed: he was buried on Iona.

Mac Bethad mac Findlàech (Macbeth)
House of Dunkeld
1005–1057 (r. 1040–1057)

Mac Bethad mac Findlàech was the son of Findlàech mac Ruaidrí, sub-king of Moray, and the grandson of Máel Coluim mac Cináeda (Malcolm II). He became sub-king of Moray when his cousin (who had succeeded his father) Gille Coemgáin died, maybe murdered, in 1032; Mac Bethad then married Coemgáin's widow, Princess Gruoch, the great granddaughter of Cináed mac Duib (Kenneth III), and became step father to her son Lulach–a possible rival for the throne of Alba.

Mac Bethad was ambitious for his cousin Donnchad mac Crínáin's (Duncan I) throne (about the only thing Shakespeare got right) and by 1040 had allied with another cousin, Earl Thorfinn of Orkney. The three met in

battle near Elgin in August 1040 and Donnchad mac Crínáin was killed leaving Mac Bethad uncontested king. Donnchad's wife and children (including two future kings) fled to safety.

Mac Bethad established his rule and stabilized the country, which allowed the economy to improve; all contemporary chronicles have nothing but praise for his reign, only later works branded him a tyrant. He even made a pilgrimage to Rome for a few months in 1050 where it was noted that he was generous to the poor. During the English battles between Edward the Confessor and Godwin, Earl of Wessex, Mac Bethad sheltered various Norman exiles from harm; it has been suggested that they introduced him to the concept of feudalism.

Above: Macbeth became legendary thanks to William Shakespeare. *Scottish Tourist Board via Jo St. Mart*

By 1054 Edward was ready to act and sent Siward, Earl of Northumbria with a large army to invade Scotland; Donnchad mac Crínáin's son Malcolm Canmore allied with the Earl of Northumbria and together they took and occupied much of southern Scotland.

Mac Bethad met the invaders in August 1057 when he was beaten in a last stand at the Battle of Lumphanan, Aberdeenshire and mortally wounded by Máel Coluim mac Donnchada (the future Malcolm III). He either died there or sixty miles away at Scone a few days later. Mac Bethad was buried on Iona and became the last of the kings of Alba to rest there.

Edgar the Aetheling when William the Conqueror had taken the English throne: they had eight children together who, significantly, were given Anglo-Saxon names.

Margaret (later cannonized as Saint Margaret of Scotland) introduced many changes: the language at court changed from Gaelic to Anglo-Saxon, one effect of which was that Máel was the first monarch to be called the King of Scotland. Further, Margaret promoted the establishment of the Roman Catholic church in Scotland over the existing Celtic Church and established

Above left: Queen Margaret was the second wife of Malcolm III. Although English, she was later cannonized as St. Margaret of Scotland. *Scottish Tourist Board via Jo St. Mart*

Above: A stained glass window in Iona Abbey showing Queen Margaret. *Scottish Tourist Board via Jo St. Mart*

Máel Coluim mac Donnchada (Malcolm III Canmore) House of Dunkeld 1030–1093 (r. 1058–1093)

Máel Coluim mac Donnchada was the son of Donnchad mac Crínáin (Duncan I) and the first king of the House of Dunkeld. He was only about nine when his father was murdered by Mac Bethad mac Findlàech (Macbeth) and went with his mother and siblings for refuge to his relatives in Northumbria. King Edward the Confessor of England supported his claim to his father's throne and invaded south Scotland in 1053 where Máel and the Earl of Northumbria joined his army which then met and killed Mac Bethad at the Battle of Lumphanan.

Mac Bethad's stepson Lulach was king for a year before being killed by Máel who then became king himself; he was crowned at Scone in April 1058. Máel's first wife was Ingibjörg and they had three sons before she died and Máel remarried in 1070. His second wife, Margaret, was the great-niece of his ally Edward the Confessor, who had sought refuge in Scotland with a group of English exiles including her brother

Dumfermline Abbey. Máel was happy to disrupt the Norman Conquest of England using the excuse of attempting to get his brother-in-law Edgar the Aetheling, his rightful throne. To this end he made repeated invasions of northern England but was driven back each time until 1072 when he was forced to sign the Treaty of Abernethy and submit to the Conqueror. Máel invaded England again after William died but was killed instead in Northumberland at the Battle of Alnwick on November 13, 1093. He was aged 62 and had ruled for 35 years: his oldest son from his second marriage, Prince Edward of Scotland, also died there. Máel's widow, Margaret, died three days later after hearing of their deaths.

Alaxandair mac Maíl Coluim (Alexander I)
House of Dunkeld
c. 1078–1124 (r. 1107–1124)

The fourth son of Máel Coluim mac Donnchada (Malcolm III) and Saint Margaret and brother-in-law of Henry I of England, he was called Alexander the Fierce. Although known as a generally pious king–he founded the abbeys at Scone and Inchcol–Alaxandair carried out terrible reprisals on his enemies from Moray and Mearns for daring to challenge him. In 1114 he led part of Henry I's campaign against the Welsh and later married his illegitimate daughter Sybilla. Alaxandair died in Stirling in 1124.

Alaxandair mac Alaxandair (Alexander III)
House of Dunkeld
1241–1286 (r. 1107–1124)

Alaxandair succeeded his father Alaxandair II to the throne of Scotland aged eight leaving the government during his minority to a series of feuding nobles. Age 21 in 1262 he took the reins of power and immediately laid claim to the Western Isles (his father's particular cause) from King Haakon of Norway which he eventually got along with the Isle of Man via the Treaty of Perth (1266): Norway kept Orkney and Shetland. In 1251 Alaxandair married Margaret of England, the daughter of King Henry III and together they had

Above: Late 18th century rendition of Colin Fitzgerald saving Alexander III from a stag. *via Jo St Mart*

Left: Coronation of Alexander III on Moot Hill, Scone. The royal poet is saying "Benach de re Albanne" (God bless the king of Scotland). *via Jo St Mart*

three children before she died in 1274. All his children predeceased him so he made Margaret, the Maid of Norway his heir. Alaxandair remarried in 1285 to Yolande de Dreux, but died, aged 44, after falling from his horse during appalling weather in Fife in 1286.

Maighread (Margaret) the Maid of Norway
House of Fairhair
1283–1290 (r. 1286–1290)

Heiress to her grandfather the childless Alaxandair mac Alaxandair (Alexander III), Maighread was a Norwegian princess; her claim was through her mother Margaret, the daughter of Alaxandair III of Scotland–her father was King Erik II of Norway. When Alaxandair died in 1286 she became queen, aged three, and guardians were appointed to rule for her. Robert Bruce, 5th Lord of Annandale and his son Robert (the father of King Robert Bruce) raised rebellion in southwest Scotland; the other contender was John Balliol. King Edward I supported Maighread's claim–probably intending to marry his son Edward, Prince of Wales, to her. Negotiations between all the interested parties continued while Maighread, then aged seven, started making her way to Scotland to be crowned queen. However, she died suddenly at Kirkwall in Orkney in 1290. Her body was taken back to Norway and buried in Bergen. She was the last of the Canmore dynasty. For the following six years there was no monarch while the 13 principal contenders fought for the throne.

John de Balliol

House of Ballol
c. 1249–1314 (r. 1292–1296)

John de Balliol was the son of wealthy English and Scottish nobles and laid claim to the Scottish throne through being the maternal great great great grandson of David I.

When King Edward I of England was asked by the Scottish lords in 1291 to arbitrate in the "Great Cause" (between the various claimants to the throne of Scotland) he chose John de Balliol. He was crowned the following year but proved little more than an English puppet. Because of this, a council was appointed to rule in his stead, and the council concluded a treaty of mutual alliance between Scotland and France, England's historic enemy, and started the "Auld Alliance."

The Wars of Scottish Independence started when a furious Edward marched his army north. After taking Dunbar John was forced to abdicate in 1296, taken to London, and imprisoned in the Tower of London before being allowed to seek shelter in France. He eventually settled at his family estates at Hélicourt in Picardy, where he died in 1314.

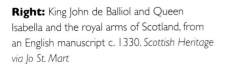

Right: King John de Balliol and Queen Isabella and the royal arms of Scotland, from an English manuscript c. 1330. *Scottish Heritage via Jo St. Mart*

Robert I the Bruce

House of Bruce
1274–1329 (r. 1306–1329)

The powerful Bruce family had laid claim to the Scottish throne since the early 13th century: on his father's side he was Norman-Scottish, on his mother's Scots-Gael. Robert Bruce was the first child of Robert de Brus, 6th Lord Annandale, and Marjorie, Countess of Carrick, and claimed the throne of Scotland as a fourth generation great grandson of Dabíd mac Maíl Choluim (David I). Despite his ancestry the Bruce family claim to the throne of Scotland—in the person of Robert de Brus, 5th Lord of Annandale—had been passed over in favor of John Balliol in 1292.

In 1296 Robert Bruce and a number of powerful Scottish nobles revolted against the English rule of Edward I. However, the English king prevailed in battle and forced the nobles to swear to the Capitulation of Irvine (1297) which established their fealty to Edward in return for their pardon and exclusion from service overseas.

But Scottish resistance continued: in September 1297 following the victory of Stirling Bridge when William Wallace and Andrew de Moray defeated the English forces, Bruce changed sides to support the Scottish cause, yet afterward he was one of the few Scottish nobles

Left: Robert I (aka Robert the Bruce) with his wife Queen Isabel, from an English manuscript c. 1330. *Scottish Heritage via Jo St. Mart*

Above: Robert the Bruce at the Battle of Bannockburn, a great victory against the English. *Scottish Heritage via Jo St. Mart*

who did not have his lands confiscated by Edward I. Wallace was defeated at the Battle of Falkirk (1297) and resigned as Guardian of Scotland, in his place Robert Bruce and John Comyn of Badeboch were made joint guardians. This was never going to work as the two families were sworn enemies and continued a generations-long feud for control of Scotland and the throne, accordingly, in 1299, a third neutral guardian, William Lamberton, Bishop of St. Andrews was appointed, but Bruce resigned the following year.

In 1295 Robert had married Isabella of Mar, the daughter of the Earl of Mar, but she died within about five years after giving birth to their daughter, Marjorie.

So, in 1302 he remarried, to Elizabeth de Burgh, daughter of the Earl of Ulster: they had four children together.

In January 1302 a truce was signed between Edward I of England and the Scottish nobles, including Bruce who had changed sides again, pledging themselves to the English king. In 1303 Edward I invaded Scotland yet again and following his successful campaign all the Scottish nobles with the exception of William Wallace submitted to him in 1304. English rule was established over Scotland and all immediate resistance disappeared with the capture and execution of Wallace in August 1305.

Robert Bruce had become the second most powerful noble in Scotland,

with huge estates scattered around the country, plus some English holdings, and a good claim to the throne. However his bitter rival John Comyn was even more powerful with more extensive estates and higher placed relatives in addition to a very strong claim on the throne. Among most Scots the latter was preferred for being loyal to their cause, unlike Robert who for political expediency continually swopped sides with the result that neither the English nor the Scots entirely trusted him.

Above: It is said that the heart of Robert
the Bruce lies here at Melrose Abbey.
Scottish Tourist Board via Jo St. Mart

In February 1306 Bruce and John
Comyn met under truce on neutral
ground in the Church of the Grey Friars
in Dumfries to discuss the situation. The
argument got heated until Bruce
stabbed and badly wounded Comyn in
front of the high altar: Bruce left swiftly,
telling his supporters—including Roger
de Kilpatrick—what had happened and
two of them went back into the church
to finish Comyn off.

In the light of events Bruce had no
option but to continue his plans to
revolt. He moved first to wipe out the
main opposition and went against the
Comyns in southern Scotland. He then
needed support from the Scottish
church, so he confessed his crime to the
Bishop of Glasgow who granted him
absolution on condition that Bruce
would respect the church when he
became king.

Robert the Bruce was crowned
Robert I at Scone in March 1306 and
Scotland was plunged into civil war as
the Comyn family opposed Bruce's rule.
Edward I, eager to destabilize Scotland
further, supported the Comyns with his
army and persuaded Pope Clement V to
excommunicate Bruce for the murder of
John Comyn.

After losing two battles many of
Bruce's supporters were dea; most of his
family members were killed or
imprisoned. His wife, Elizabeth de
Burgh, was not killed but imprisoned in
Yorkshire because she was the daughter
of an ally of Edward's, but his mistress,
Isabella, Countess of Buchan, was
confined in an open cage over the
battlements of Berwick Castle. Robert
meanwhile went into hiding through
the winter of 1306–07, probably on
Rathlin Island off the Irish coast. He
returned to Scotland in February 1307
and after a couple of skirmishes his
army of 600 defeated the English army
of 3,000 at Loudon Hill—with this he
won popular support across Scotland.

Then, in July 1307, Edward I died
near Solway Firth, and the English lost
their driving force as his less capable
son became King Edward II. Robert the
Bruce continued his guerilla tactics
across southern Scotland, attacking the
Comyns and their supporters in
particular, but also his other enemies
and anyone who supported the English.
Castle after castle fell to him. In May
1308 his army devastated Buchan
burning every village and killing every
Comyn they found. They took Aberdeen
and slaughtered the English garrison
then turned to take the last Comyn
stronghold, Dunstaffnage Castle. By the
end of that year Robert Bruce controlled
almost all of northern Scotland and a
year later controlled all Scotland north
of the River Tay.

1309 saw the clergy finally accepting
Robert Bruce as king of Scotland and he
held his first parliament that March.
Over the next five years he recaptured
strongholds from English hands:

Linlithgow (1310), Dumbarton (1311), Perth (1313), Roxburgh (1313), and finally Edinburgh (1314), as well as constant plundering raids over the English border. However, the English still held Stirling Castle despite a prolonged siege.

In 1314 Edward II took his army of 20,000 soldiers into Scotland where they encountered an army of 7,000 Scots at Bannockburn on June 24, 1314. After desperate fighting on both sides the Scots prevailed: the English tried to flee and many of their knights were slaughtered, Edward II only just managed to escape. Bruce captured the Earl of Hereford who he exchanged for his wife, sister, and daughter. Scottish raids continued over the border with even greater success.

On April 6, 1320 the Scots declared their independence with the Declaration of Arbroath. This document announced their nationhood under King Robert I and was sent to Pope John XXII, who arranged a truce with England and peace talks started the following year. Although the talks broke down and the Scottish raids resumed, the pope formally accepted Robert the Bruce as king of Scotland. Edward II died, probably murdered, and Edward III became king of England.

The raids continued until in March 1328 when the Treaty of Edinburgh–Northampton was signed, Edward renounced all English claims to sovereignty over Scotland and Robert in

Left: Statue of Robert the Bruce at Stirling Castle. *Scottish Tourist Board via Jo St. Mart*

return paid England 20,000 marks compensation for damage done during the border raids into England. To seal the treaty, a marriage was arranged between Bruce's four-year-old son David (future David II) and Edward III's seven-year-old sister, Joan of England. The marriage ceremony was held in July 1328 and Robert the Bruce died a little less than a year later on June 7, 1329, at Dumbarton, from what was described as an "unclean ailment." He was buried at Dunfermline Abbey.

An unconfirmed legend says that his heart was removed and taken on crusade as far as Granada in Spain and returned some years later to be buried with him.

Daibhidh a Briuis
(David II)

House of Bruce
1324–1371 (r. 1329–1371)

Daibhidh had already married Joan of the Tower (Princess Joanna of England) daughter of Edward II (and sister of Edward III) in 1328, a year before he became king of Scotland (age five) on the death of his father Robert the Bruce (Robert I). When he was nine years old Daibhidh and his queen were sent to France where they spent the following eight years in exile while Edward Balliol (c.1282–1364) was king of Scotland.

Daibhidh returned to Scotland to rule in his own name when his followers were victorious in 1341. In 1346 to honor his commitment to the Auld Alliance he invaded England but

following defeat at the Battle of Neville's Cross (1346) he was captured and taken back to England for the next eleven years. Following the Treaty of Berwick upon Tweed (1357) and on the agreement of a ransom of 100,000 marks he returned to Scotland: however, only part of the money was handed over so Daibhidh offered to make Edward III his heir instead.

Above: David II of Scotland and Edward III of England agree the Treaty of Berwick in 1357. *Scottish Heritage via Jo St. Mart*

Daibhidh died in Edinburgh Castle in 1371, he left no children and so ended the male line of the House of Bruce.

Robert II
House of Stewart
1316–1390 (r. 1371–1390)

The first king of the House of Stewart was the son of Walter Stewart and Marjorie Bruce, daughter of Robert I. While Robert I's son Daibhidh a Briuis reigned, Robert Stewart became a leading martial noble fighting for the Scottish king and was one of the regents in charge of the kingdom while Daibhidh a Briuis (David II) lived for safety in France.

When the regents fell out with each other Robert became sole regent and controlled the situation so well that Daibhidh was able to return to his throne in 1341. But when Daibhidh was captured after the Battle of Neville's Cross (1346) and confined to England, Robert–who had escaped from the battle–once again became regent.

When, in 1363, Robert suspected that Daibhidh was making Edward III of England his heir, he revolted: he was caught and quickly released and soon after declared king when Daibhidh died without leaving children. He was crowned in March 1371 age 55 and reigned for 19 years.

A riding accident saw his health deteriorate markedly, and the Scottish Parliament appointed his second son Robert, Earl of Fife as his heir in 1389.

Robert II died at Dundonald in 1390, he fathered 21 children, not all of them legitimate (thanks to the laws of consanguinity).

Above: Robert II was the first king from the House of Stewart (later spelled Stuart). *Scottish Heritage via Jo St. Mart*

James I
House of Stewart
1394–1437 (r. 1406–1437)

Son of Robert III and Annabella Drummond, while a child he was sent to France for his own safety to keep him away from jealous relatives. But instead he was captured and handed over to Henry IV of England who demanded a ransom for his return. James's father died in 1406–rumor said from grief–and his uncle Robert Stewart became regent but failed to find the ransom money for James' release (although he did for his own son). James remained a hostage in England for the next 18 years. When Robert Stewart died in 1420 the Scottish nobles raised the £40,000 ransom and secured his return in 1424. Meanwhile James married Joan Beaufort, a cousin of Henry VI: they had eight children.

On his return James had his uncle's family executed and ruthlessly set about ordering his chaotic kingdom–the clan feuds in the Highlands were worse than ever and the Border barons uncontrollable–making numerous financial and legal reforms. He also renewed the Auld Alliance in 1428. But as time progressed questions about his legitimacy arose and James was assassinated in front of his wife by a group of eight Scottish nobles led by Sir Robert Graham at the Friars Preachers Monastery in Perth. The queen vowed revenge and soon the killers were hunted down and tortured before being executed.

James II
House of Stewart
1430–1460 (r. 1437–1460)

The younger of twin sons of James I of Scotland and Joan Beaufort, his brother died in infancy. James II became king at the age of seven when his father was assassinated in 1437. His father's usurpers, particularly Walter Stewart, 1st Earl of Atholl, tried to capture the throne but were executed within

Right and Far right: James I spent 18 years as a hostage in England and only returned home—with an English bride—after a huge ransom was paid. He was an effective monarch who organized much of the workings of early Scottish government. *Hulton Archive/Getty Images; Scottish Heritage via Jo St. Mart*

months. Between 1437 and 1439 Archibald Douglas, 5th Earl of Douglas ruled as regent, when he died a series of other Scottish nobles attempted to rule and power swopped from noble to noble. In 1449 James came into his majority but continued to struggle against a number of Scottish nobles—especially the Douglases—for power. Then, in 1452, at Stirling Castle, James stabbed the 8th Earl of Douglas to death, causing intermittent civil war for the next three years. The Douglases were finally defeated at the Battle of Arkinholm in May 1455; those who survived fled to exile in England and all Douglas lands were confiscated, mostly to the crown. James was not seriously challenged again.

In 1460 during the successful siege of Roxburgh Castle (still in English hands) a canon exploded and killed James II; he was 29.

James III
House of Stewart
c. 1452–1488 (r. 1460–1488)

James became king at the age of nine on the death of his father James II. His mother, Mary of Guelders, ruled as regent until she died in 1463. He was crowned in 1460 at Kelso Abbey.

In 1469 James took his full royal authority and married Princess Margaret of Denmark. When her dowry from her father King Christian I of Denmark defaulted, he acquired for the Scottish crown Orkney and Shetland in compensation.

James became estranged from his brothers the Duke of Albany and John, Earl of Mar, who despised James' love of the arts and his cordial relations with England; in 1479 Mar died in suspicious circumstances and Albany fled to England (then France) as their supporters scattered.

By 1486 James was an isolated figure living in Stirling Castle. Two years later at the Battle of Sauchieburn James was thrown from his horse and died; alternatively the story goes that while lying injured in a nearby cottage, a "priest" came to shrive him but instead stabbed him to death.

Far left and Left:

James II was known as "James of the fiery face" because of a birthmark. *Hulton Archive/Getty Images 51243673; Scottish Heritage via Jo St. Mart*

Right and Far right:

Crowned in 1460, the country was run by a succession of regents during James III's minority. *Hulton Archive/Getty Images 51243748; Scottish Heritage via Jo St. Mart (Window in Kirkwall town Hall, Orkney)*

James IV
House of Stewart
1473–1513 (r. 1488–1513)

During the second popular rebellion against his father James III, 15-year-old James was proclaimed as their leader. When James III was killed at the Battle of Sauchieburn in June 1488, James became king. He proved a much better ruler than his father and through his own interest in administration and justice stabilized his kingdom; additionally he established peace with England with the Treaty of Perpetual Peace (1502) with Henry VII, which also authorized his marriage to Margaret Tudor–the marriage of The Thisle and the Rose (1503). He also built the Scottish navy and was a great patron of the arts and sciences.

In 1513 when Henry VIII of England joined the Holy Alliance and invaded France, James–constrained by the Auld Alliance to support France–declared

Above left: James IV was the last British king killed in battle at Flodden Field in 1513. *Scottish Heritage via Jo St. Mart*

Above: James IV on horseback. *The Art Archive/Bibliothèque des Arts Décoratifs Paris/ Gianni Dagli Orti*

Above right: The large stained-glass window at the south end of Parliament Hall, which depicts the inauguration of the Court of Session by King James V in 1532, *Scottish Parliament via Jo St. Mart*

James V

House of Stewart
1512–1542 (r. 1513–1542)

James became king of Scotland when aged one after his father James IV was killed at the Battle of Flodden Field in 1513. For one year his English mother, Margaret Tudor, ruled as regent but the Scottish nobles deposed her when she remarried in 1514. Their choice as regent was the Duke of Albany (next but one in line for the throne). James's step-father, the 6th Earl of Angus was soon divorced by Margaret, but he kidnapped young James and then held him in captivity for two years while he tried to corrupt him with luxuries and gifts and ruled on his behalf. Despite this James hated him and managed to escape in 1528 and become king on his own. He exacted revenge on his opponents, especially the Earl of Angus whom he exiled.

Although he married twice, none of his legitimate children survived infancy although his nine or so illegitimate children were fine. After failing to meet his uncle King Henry VIII as arranged at York in 1542, James had to march south with his army to counter the furious English king's invasion force. The Battle of Solway Moss in November 1542 was a heavy defeat for the Scots. Already ill, James suffered a complete nervous breakdown; he took to his bed at Falkland Palace with a fever where he heard the dispiriting news that his wife had borne a daughter, Mary (Queen of Scots). Six days later, fearing the Stewart dynasty finished, he died.

war on England and invaded. At the subsequent Battle of Flodden Field in September 1513, many Scopttish nobles were killed alongside king James–the last British monarch to die in battle. He was also the last Scottish king known to have spoken Scottish Gaelic.

Left: James IV and Queen Margaret, daughter of King Henry VII of England from a Manuscript of the Arms of the Nobility of Scotland, 1588. *The Art Archive/Bodleian Library Oxford Wood C.9 fol.13r AA382026*

Mary I Queen of Scots

House of Stuart
1542–1587 (r. 1542–1567)

Above: Depiction of the Battle of Langside, 1568. *The Art Archive/Galleria d'Arte Moderna Milan/Gianni Dagli Orti AA367804*

Mary Stewart was born at Linlithgow Palace in West Lothian to James V and Mary of Guise and became queen of Scotland at six days old when her father died of cholera without other heirs. She was the great-granddaughter of King Henry VII of England, which made her next in line to the throne after King Henry VIII's children. To secure her and Scotland's future the Scottish nobles agreed a marriage between Mary and Henry VIII's son Edward (the future King Edward VI) in the Treaties of Greenwich. However, the Scottish Catholic nobles and her mother, Mary of Guise, were opposed to an English Protestant alliance with their young queen and spirited her off to Stirling Castle.

Henry VIII was furious at the change of policy and ordered the "Rough Wooing," a series of savage raids across the border into Scotland. Crops were burned across the Tweed Valley, and the abbeys of Jedburgh, Dryburgh, Melrose, and Holyroodhouse were burned down. The Scots appealed to the French for help and Henri II proposed a marriage between five-year-old Mary and his three-year-old son, the Dauphin of France, Francis. The marriage treaty was agreed in 1548.

August that same year Mary, Queen of Scots, and her small retinue of courtiers was sent to live at the French court. She remained there for 13 years during which time she was well educated and became a popular member of court. She changed the spelling of her name during this period from Stewart to the more French, Stuart. The marriage took place in Paris in April 1558 and the following year Francis succeeded his father to the throne and Mary became queen consort of France. However, within two years Francis died of an ear infection and aged 17 Mary became a widow in 1560.

In August 1561 and against all advice, Catholic Mary returned to her Scottish throne despite Scotland having officially converted to Protestantism following John Knox's reforms. She had been assured that she would be allowed to worship as she wished. Initially her return was welcomed and with the advice of her chief advisor Lord James Stuart (Protestant) her reign was uncontroversial.

Four years into her return Mary married her second cousin Henry Stuart, Lord Darnley, who was—as was Mary—a great grandchild of King Henry VII of England. Darnley was a disastrous choice; he wanted to be treated as the king and his arrogance quickly made enemies and conspirators were only too happy to use him for their own ends. Then, in March 1566 at Holyroodhouse Palace, Darnley burst into the heavily pregnant queen's chamber, threatened her and in a jealous rage murdered her secretary David Riccio before her eyes.

Their son James was born in June that summer but their relationship had irretrievably broken down; when Darnley was murdered just outside Edinburgh in Februaury 1567, Mary was widely suspected of complicity. When Mary married James Hepburn, 4th Earl of Bothwell, the prime suspect in the murder, her remaining creditability vanished. Her Protestant nobles raised an army against her and when they met Mary and Bothwell at Carberry Hill in June 1567 Mary had no choice but to surrender. She was imprisoned in Lochleven Castle and forced to abdicate in favor of her one-year-old son James. Bothwell fled to Scandinavia where he was arrested and held prisoner until he died in 1578.

In 1568 Mary managed to escape from Lochleven, but her army was defeated at the Battle of Langside in May. Without friends in Scotland Mary fled to England in the belief that her cousin Queen Elizabeth would support her; but Mary was too dangerous as the Catholic contender for the throne of England and instead Elizabeth imprisoned her for 19 years. In England Mary became the center of Catholic plots to put her on the throne. How much she knew or encouraged such treason is unknown. Elizabeth was unwilling to execute her but, following Mary's almost certain involvement in the Babington Plot to assassinate Elizabeth, even the queen could no longer ignore her ministers' advice to remove Mary altogether.

Mary had her head chopped off at Fotheringhay Castle in Northamptonshire in February 1587. She was 44. She was initially buried in Peterborough Cathedral, but her son James VI had her remains removed to Henry VII's chapel in Westminster Abbey.

Right: Mary was notable for her disastrous choices of husbands and lovers which helped her ruin. *Wikipedia via Jo St. Mart*

Welsh Princes

Much of early Welsh history is hidden in a morass of myth and mystery; written records are few and far between and are rarely reliable. The very landscape dictated the political development of Wales as the treacherous weather and high mountains conspired to keep rival tribes from each other. For centuries Wales was a patchwork of principalities, warrior leaders, and kings who occasionally conquered and forcibly united rival territories under a powerful leader and then were immediately riven as soon as weaker successors followed. Largely because the Welsh lands were not cohesively united under one strong ruler, English King Edward I was able to impose his rule and absorb Wales into his dominions.

The Welsh have their own Celtic-rooted language and in their own tongue call their land Cymru. People have lived there since the end of the last Iron Age, about 9,000 years ago. After the Romans conquered much of mainland Britian they encountered fierce resistance in the mountains and only partially conquered Wales. After the Romans left Britian, Welsh warlords established the kingdoms of Powys and Gwynedd alongside other much smaller and more transient kingdoms which appeared and

disappeared as their more powerful neighbors conquered and lost lands. During the medieval period the Welsh kingdom of Gwynedd (a large portion of northwest Wales) became the pre-eminent power in the land and the ruler self-styled himself as the King of the Britons.

Historically the Welsh and the English—mostly in the form of the kingdom of Mercia—have continually fought each other for power and political influence, with the upper hand varying with the intelligence and strength of the local leaders. The situation changed with the Norman Conquest of England in 1066 as the whole of Albion was subjugated to the Norman yoke: after England was subdued, Norman attention turned to Wales.

It took time, but by the death of Llwelyn the Last in 1282, Wales too became subjugated to Norman rule. King Edward I built a string of huge stone castles across the land to enforce his will and impose Anglo-Norman rule over Wales. Today they are great tourist traps with Harlech, Conwy, and Caernarfon the most prestigious. Edward I's son who later became Edward II was born here in 1284. It is said Edward I promised the conquered Welsh a prince who could speak not a word of English—they accepted and

were furious when they were presented with his infant son as their Prince of Wales. Edward was given the title and it has been bestowed on every first-born son of the monarch ever since.

Welsh resistance to the English crown did not cease with Edward I's reign. Sporadic resistance, notably from Owain Glyndwr in the early 15th century, revived Welsh hopes of

employment and a measure of prosperity to the land. Welshmen joined the British army and Welsh adventurers and empire builders shared in the new wealth and power produced by the growth and spread of the British Empire. Through all the colonial battles and then two bitter World Wars, Welshmen and women fought alongside their English, Irish, and Scottish comrades.

From the mid-20th century the political hot potato of devolution (political separation from the rest of the United Kingdom) became a driving concern; the first popular referendum in 1979 returned a "no" vote, but a second in 1997 produced a narrow "yes." Consequently, the separate Welsh Assembly was established in Cardiff with legislative powers over Wales–the parliament in Westminster still decides matters of national interest.

The few leaders covered in this section give a taste of the lives of some of the important figures in Welsh history.

I've used the general term "princes" rather than monarchy as a chapter heading because because monarchy implies overlordship of a country: many of the Welsh princes may have aspired to be ruler of Wales but few, if any, united the parts into a whole.

independence, but ultimately failed, as much from inter-Welsh rivalries and the inability to unite under one strong leader as fromAnglo-Norman strength.

In the 16th century Wales was fully and completely incorporated into England with the Laws in Wales Acts 1535–42, but by then a Welsh Tudor dynasty sat on the throne of England. From then on the two countries shared similar ambitions and desires although despite this the Welsh language and culture remained strong and notably different from the rest of Britain, although sharing strong Celtic roots with parts of Ireland, Scotland, and the west of England.

With the arrival of the Industrial Revolution in the 19th century Wales saw a huge rise in population and increase in industrialization as the coal mines and smelting industries brought

Left: Y Ddraig Goch—the red dragon—has symbolized Wales for hundreds of years but was only officially adopted in 1959.

Rhodri the Great

(Rhodri ap Merfyn)

King of Gwynedd
c. 820–878

Born the son of Merfyn Frych, King of Gwynedd and Nest ferch Cadell from the royal house of Powys, Rhodri was born in about 820, but unfortunately very little is known about him. He inherited the kingdom of Gwynedd from his father in 844 and then Powys from his uncle in 855. He married Angharad of Seisyllwg and inherited her family lands when her brother Gwgon of Seisyllwg drowned in 872. Rhodri then ruled most of Wales.

This was the era of the Viking raiders who ravaged the entire British Isles and Rhodri's kingdom was under attack, with one particularly damaging raid on Anglesey in 854. The other constant threat was from his Wessex neighbors. Rhodri was a great warrior and won a famous victory against the Danes in 856 when he killed the Danish leader Gorm (or Horn); this won him international acclaim and attention. Rhodri now ruled from Anglesey to the Gower peninsula.

Rhodri was not so successful in 876 in another battle on Anglesey against the Danes and had to flee to Ireland. He returned the following year and was probably killed in battle against Alfred the Great. His sons, Anarawd, King of Gwynedd and Powys, and Cadell, King of Seisyllwg in time had to submit to Alfred the Great and acknowledge him as their overlord. To be descended from Rhodri Mawr's bloodline became the most important qualification to rule Wales.

Hywel the Good
(Hywel Dda)
King of Deheubarth
c. 880–950

Hywel ap Cadell ap Rhodri, better known as Hywel Dda, was the grandson of Rhodri the Great and was born in about 880 but whereabouts unknown. In 905 his father, Cadell ap Rhodri, gave him newly conquered Dyfed to rule on his behalf. As part of the settlement Hywel married Elen, the daughter of Llywarch ap Hyfaidd the former ruler of Dyfed.

When Cadell ap Rhodri died in 909 Hywel inherited part of Seisyllwg kingdom in south Wales (Ceredigion and Ystrad Tywi), and when his brother Clydog died in 920 Hywel created the new kingdom of Deheubarth in southwest Wales. In 930 he added Brycheiniog, then Powys, and finally Gwynedd when his cousin Idwal Foel died in battle against the English in 942. He was now "King of all Wales."

Hywel's contemporary across the border in England was Athelstan, whom he pragmatically acknowleged as his overlord and to whom he paid tribute: they formed a strong alliance and possibly even a friendship, in any event they jointly ruled parts of Wales. Hywel became the first Welsh ruler to mint his own coins (at Chester in England) in over a thousand years. Particularly interested in law and legal systems, Hywel even visited Rome in 928 and on his return produced his own law book. In 945 the Whitland conference codified Welsh law (the Laws of Hywel Dda) and wrote it down for posterity–it was not abolished until the 16th century.

When Hywel died his kingdom included all of modern Wales except what is now Glamorgan and Gwent. This wasn't to last; when Hywel died the kingdom was split into three: Deheubarth divided between his sons, and Gwynedd reclaimed by the sons of Idwal Foel.

Left: Statue of Hywel the Good by F.W. Pomeroy in Cardiff City Hall. *via Jo St. Mart*

Gruffydd ap Llywelyn
Prince of Gwynedd
c. 1007–1063

Gruffyd ap Llywelyn was the eldest son of the ruler of Gwynedd and Powys, Llywelyn ap Seisyll and his wife Angharad. Instead of inheriting his father's kingdom on his death in 1023 it went instead to Iago ap Idwal who ruled until being killed by his own supporters in 1039–possibly with the connivance of Gruffyd. Meanwhile, Gruffyd had taken power in Powys and siezed his opportunity to take Gwynedd on Iago's death.

Gruffydd was aggressively intent on extending his kingdom–he was well known to be ruthless and bloodthirsty–and attacked and took neighboring Deheubarth from Hywel ap Edwin in about 1043 at the Battle of Aber Tywi but was driven out again in 1047 by Gruffydd ap Rhydderch of Gwent.

Next he attacked towns along the Welsh border around Herefordshire. In 1055 the two Gruffyds met in battle with Gruffyd ap Llywelyn killing Gruffydd ap Rhydderch and retaking Deheubarth.

With his new English ally Aelfgar (son of the desposed Earl of East Anglia, Earl Leofric of Mercia) he marched on Hereford and there defeated the Earl of Hereford. The victors sacked the city and destroyed the castle. Soon after Aelfgar was restored to the earldom and a peace treaty was agreed. In addition he married Ealdgyth, Aelfgar's daughter; in 1055 Aelfgar became Earl of Mercia and an even more powerful ally for Gruffyd.

Back in Wales Gruffydd took Morgannwg and Gwent by force and much of the Welsh border country and claimed sovereignty over Wales–and reached an accord with Edward the Confessor who recognized his authority. But his old ally Aelfgar died in 1062, leaving Gruffydd's position exposed. His vulnerability was recognized by Harold Godwinson who made a surprise midwinter attack with support from southern Welsh fighters on Gruffydd's court at Rhuddlan; Gruffydd was warned to escape just in time. In the following spring Harold attacked south Wales while his brother Tostig took his army into north Wales. Gruffydd fled to Snowdonia where he and his men were trapped. On August 5, 1063, Gruffyd was killed by his own men and his head sent to Harold as proof of his

death and a sign of their submission; however, the Ulster Chronicle stated that Gruffydd was killed by Cynan ap Iago, in revenge for the killing of his father Iago ab Idwal in 1039. Gruffydd's kingdoms split back into their traditional disunity instead of to his eldest son Dafydd and his widow Ealdgyth married Harold Godwinson.

Llywelyn the Great
(Llywelyn ap Iorwerth or Llwelyn Fawr)
Prince of Gwynedd
c. 1172–1240

Llywelyn ap Iorwerth was the son of Iorwerth ap Owain of the ruling family of Gwynedd and Marared, daughter of Madog ap Maredudd, prince of Powys. He was probably born at Dolwyddelan. During Llywelyn's childhood Gwynedd was divided between his uncles Dafydd ab Owain and Rhodri ab Owain, but Llywelyn also had a good claim and it is probable that he was fighting them for Gwynedd as early as 1188. Six years later, and with the help of his cousins Gruffudd ap Cynan and Maredudd ap Cynan he defeated his uncle Dafydd in battle at Aberconwy and then Rhodri died in 1195. Llywelyn took lands east of the Conwy and his cousins' took the lands west of the Conwy.

Under Rhys ap Gruffydd Deheubarth had been the strongest Welsh kingdom, but on his death it was split up leaving Llywelyn an opportunity to establish

Above: Statue of Llywelyn ap Gruffydd. *via Jo St. Mart*

Left: Statue of Gruffydd ap Llywelyn in Cardiff City Hall. *via Jo St. Mart*

himself as the strongest independent Welsh leader. By 1199 he had captured the castle of Mold and was calling himself "prince of the whole of North Wales," an exaggeration until his cousin Gruffudd ap Cynan died in 1200 leaving Llywelyn the undisputed leader in Gwynedd.

In July 1200 Llywelyn made a treaty with King John of England and swore fealty to him–the earliest known written agreement between the rulers of England and Wales. The treaty confirmed Llywelyn's conquests and allowed him to hear land claims under Welsh law. His main court was at Garth Celyn in north Gwynedd and it remained the effective capital of Wales until medieval times.

Llywelyn's principal rival was Gwenwynwyn ab Owain, prince of Powys Wenwynwyn, and self-proclaimed leader of the Welsh princes; both men desperately wanted each other's possessions but neither was strong enough to take the other until in 1205 Llywelyn strengthened his status by marrying Joan, the illegitimate daughter of King John of England. Three years later King John argued with Gwenwynwyn, had him arrested and ,his lands confiscated and then turned a blind eye when Llywelyn took southern Powys and northern Ceredigion for himself. By way of thanks Llywelyn joined King John on his campaign against William I of Scotland in 1209.

However the following year John and Llywelyn fell out and the former sent his army to invade Gwynedd with the support of most of the other Welsh rulers. Llywelyn was finally forced to come to terms, and thanks to Joan's intercession with her father, he was not totally dispossessed: he lost all his lands east of the River Conwy, handed over hostages, and agreed to pay huge tribute of 20,000 cattle and 40 horses, additionally he had to agree to leave all his lands to the KIng of England if he died without a legitimate heir by Joan.

The other Welsh princes soon reneged on their alliance with John and turned to Llywelyn–Pope Innocent III had placed John and England under Interdict and was only too delighted to release all the Welsh princes from their vows of allegiance to John. By 1212 Llywelyn had recovered almost all of Gwynedd, in 1213 he took the castles of Deganwy and Rhuddlan. Then he allied himself to Philip II of France and to the barons rebelling against King John, marched on Shrewsbury and captured it. He soon held south Wales and then captured much of mid-Wales. When King John signed the Magna Carta Llywelyn received more powers and became indisputably the strongest ruler in Wales and the leader of the independent princes of Wales. In 1216 in council at Aberdovey Llywelyn took pledges of allegiance as Overlord of All from his fellow Welsh princes and adjudicated on a number of land claims, and rewarded his supporters.

By 1217 King John was dead and Henry III was on the throne of England. Llywelyn concluded the Treaty of Worcester with the new king which confirmed him in all his conquests. Nevertheless battles and arguments erupted as the lesser Welsh princes continued to swop sides and maneuver for advantage, and Llywelyn was frequently fighting with and against them, the king, and the Marcher lords. Between 1220 and 1230 Llywelyn built a number of large stone castles to defend his borders including Dolbadarn and Criccieth, and in 1230 changed his title to become Prince of Aberffraw and Lord of Snowdon. The fighting ended in June 1234 when Llywelyn and Henry concluded the Peace of Middle, a two-year truce which was continually renewed until 1240.

Llywelyn only had one legitimate son, Dafydd who he was determined would inherit his kingdom. He got the king of England's support for this, and that of the pope, and in 1238 he made the other Welsh princes to swear fealty to Dafydd.

In 1237 Joan died and Llywelyn was partially paralysed by stroke so Dafydd took on much of the process of government. Llywelyn died aged 68 and was buried at the abbey of Aberconwy in 1240 and was succeeded by Dafydd as prince of Gwynedd–King Henry did not allow him to inherit the rest of Wales. Dafydd died in 1246 without leaving an heir.

Llywelyn the Last
(Llywelyn ap Gruffydd)
Prince of Wales
c. 1223–1282

Llywelyn's father Gruffydd was the second son of Llywellyn the Great and when the latter died in 1240 Gruffydd and his brother Owain were sent as prisoners to England by his uncle Dafydd ap Llywelyn, the new Welsh king. Four years later Gruffydd died while trying to escape from a high window of the Tower of London. With his father dead and no longer a prisoner of King Henry III, Llywellyn could fight alongside his uncle against the English. In February 1246 Dafydd unexpectedly died without an heir and Llywellyn and his uncle Owain made a truce with Henry in which Gwynedd was divided between them.

Years of fighting followed with Llywelyn gradually extending his territories. In 1267 in the Treaty of Montgomery King Henry recognized Llywelyn as Prince of Wales (most of modern Wales) in return for which he

had to pay hefty tribute. But Welsh rivalries were never still and Llywellyn was never as strong again. When the new English King Edward I invited him to his coronation and then summoned Llywellyn to pay homage to him at Chester in 1275, he refused both times and made himself a powerful enemy. In 1276 Llywellyn was declared a rebel and a price was put on his head, Edward assembled an army of some 15,600 soldiers–including many of the lesser Welsh princes who resented Llywellyn's authority. Trapped and surrounded by enemies Llywellyn had to sign the Treaty of Aberconwy to guarantee peace in Gwynedd, in addition he had to pay homage to Edward and was stripped of the majority of his conquests.

Above: Statue of Owain Glyndŵr, in Cardiff City Hall. *Wikipedia via Jo St. Mart*

The situation was quietened but not settled and in 1282 many of the Welsh princes revolted: Llywellyn eventually joining them. The English army returned to Wales: after prolonged fighting across Wales Llywellyn was killed, either by treachery or possibly by chance, while separated from his army at Irfon Bridge near Builth Wells. His corpse was beheaded and the head sent to Edward at Rhuddlan and then on to London where it was paraded for the crowds to jeer at and was then mounted on a pole at the Tower of London.

Owain Glyndwr
(Owain Glyn Dwr)
Prince of Wales
c. 1354–c. 1416

One of six children of Gruffydd Fychan II and his wife Elen ferch Tomas ap Llywelyn, Glyndwr came from a prosperous Anglo-Welsh family in the Welsh Marches of northeast Wales. His father died while Owain was about 16 and the boy was sent to London to study law at the Inns of Court, probably for about seven years.

By 1383 Glyndwr had returned to Wales and married Margaret Hanmer. Hed became the squire of Sycharth and Glyndyfrdwy. Glyndwr is thought to have fathered some 15 children. In 1384 Glyndwr entered the English king's service doing garrison duty on the England-Scotland border at Berwick-on-Tweed, and in the following year fought in France, Scotland again, and England. In 1387 he returned to Wales when his father-in-law died and served as a squire to Henry Bolingbroke (later Henry IV) at the Battle of Radcot Bridge (1387). After military service, during his forties, Glyndwr lived quietly for ten years.

However, he had a long running land dispute with his Norman neighbor, Baron Grey de Ruthyn, in which King Richard and the courts found for Glyndwr. But on the accession of Henry IV Baron Grey used his friendship with the king to overturn the verdict and, crucially, did not inform Glyndwr of his Royal Summons to join the king's Scottish campaign. By not appearing, Glyndwr unknowingly committed treason: unaware of the deception King Henry declared Glyndwr a traitor and his lands forfeit and made Grey his agent. Glyndwr had no option but to revolt and fight.

On September 16, 1400 Glyndwr was proclaimed Prince of Wales by his followers–he caertainly had the best claim to the Welsh throne. The revolt swiftly and successfully spread through northeast Wales and then south; by 1401 north and central Wales belonged to Glyndwr. In response Henry appointed Henry Percy (Harry "Hotspur") to stifle the revolt and issued an amnesty to all the rebels except Glyndwr.

Glyndwr's first big victory was at the Battle of Mynydd Hyddgeb (1401) and the revolt looked likely to spread. Hotspur wanted to negotiate and stop the-repression, but anti English and anti-Welsh feelings intensified on both sides. In 1402 Glyndwr ambushed and captured Baron Grey de Ruthyn who he then ransomed and in the process ruined financially. In 1403, and with help from the French, the revolt spread across the whole of Wales. Experienced Welsh soldiers left English service to join the rebellion as did Welshmen from all over Britain. In 1403 Hotspur changed sides to support Glyndwr and challenge Henry IV's right to the throne, but he was killed at the Battle of Shrewsbury alongside some 20,000 dead or injured.

In 1404 Glyndwr captured Harlech and Aberystwyth castles, called his first *Cynulliad* (parliament) and was crowned Owain IV of Wales. He started negotiating with disaffected English lords, notably Edmund Mortimer and the Earl of Northumberland, and signed a treaty with the French that promised aid from France. Meanwhile Breton, Irish, and Scots raiders took the opportunity to wreak havoc around the English coastline. In 1405 a French expeditionary force arrived at Milford Haven and joined up with the Welsh forces in South Wales. They met the English army near Worcester–there was a standoff for eight days without any fighting, then both sides withdrew, the French and Welsh returning to Wales under cover of dark.

By 1406 most of the French had returned to France and the Welsh were losing to the English. Under the command of Henry of Monmouth trade, weapons, and supplies were slowly but surely denied the rebels and Glyndwr's supporters negotiated their own surrender terms. Despite appeals to the French, no help came. Members of Glyndwr's family were captured and imprisoned in the Tower of London where they all died.

Glyndwr was a hunted man with only scattered outposts of support. The last known sighting of Glyndwr was in 1412. The following year Henry V took the throne and with it pardons for a number of the rebels and a less harsh attitude toward the Welsh. Huge rewards were posted for Glyndwr, and in 1415 a pardon was offered to him: but nothing was heard from him and his fate remains a mystery, although he might have spent his last years in England with his daughter and her English husband in Herefordshire.

Timeline

793	Vikings attack Lindisfarne Abbey–first recorded attack
800	Danes (German tribes) start attacking Britain and Ireland
802	In Wessex Egbert accedes
825	Battle of Ellendun. Egbert defeats Mercia
829	Egbert receives submission of Northumbria
839	In Wessex Ethelwulf accedes
843	Kenneth Mac Alpin accedes to the throne of the Picts
856	In Wessex Ethelbald accedes
858	Donald I accedes to the throne of the Picts
860	In Wessex Ethelburt accedes
862	Constantine I accedes to the throne of the Picts
866	In Wessex Ethelred accedes
867	Vikings take York
871	In Wessex Alfred the Great accedes
874	Vikings conquer Mercia
877	Aed accedes to the throne of the Picts
878	Giric accedes to the throne of the Picts
878	Treaty of Wedmore splits England into two: creation of the Danelaw. Confirmed by Treaty in 866
889	Donald II accedes to the throne as "King of Scots"
899	In Wessex Edward the Elder accedes
900	Constantine accedes in Scotland
924	In Wessex Elfward accedes
925	Athelstan the Glorious accedes. First king of "All England"

939	Edmund the Magnificent follows Athelstan
943	Malcolm I accedes in Scotland
946	Edred accedes in England
954	Indulf accedes in Scotland
955	Edwy All-Fair accedes in England
959	Edgar the Peaceful accedes in England
962	Dub accedes in Scotland
967	Cuilen accedes in Scotland
971	Amlaib accedes in Scotland
975	Edward the Martyr accedes in England
977	Kenneth II accedes in Scotland
978	Ethelred II the Unready accedes in England
919	Vikings defeat northern Irish kings
950	Hywel the Good dies. Vikings forced out of York
995	Constantine III accedes in Scotland
997	Kenneth III accedes in Scotland
1005	Malcolm II accedes in Scotland
1013	Ethelred the Unready exiled by Sweyn Forkbeard
1016	Edmund Ironside accedes in England. Defeated by Canute at Battle of Ashingdon.
1034	Duncan I accedes in Scotland
1035	Harold Harefoot accedes in England as regent for Harthacanute. Defeats Edward (later Edward the Confessor)
1040	Macbeth accedes in Scotland
1040	Danish King Harthacanute accedes in England. On his death Edward the Confessor accedes restoring the Anglo-Saxon line
1057	Lulach accedes in Scotland
1058	Malcolm III accedes in Scotland
1066	Harold accedes in England. Defeats invasion by Tostig and Harald III Hardrada of Norway at Stamford Bridge. He is defeated at Battle of

	Hastings by William of Normandy who is crowned King of England
1077	Bayeux Tapestry completed
1086	Domesday Book survey of land ownership completed
1087	William II accedes in England
1091	Malcolm II invades England
1093	Donald III accedes in Scotland
1094	Duncan II accedes in Scotland
1094	Edmund accedes in Scotland
1097	Edgar accedes in Scotland
1100	Henry I accedes in England following William II's death in a hunting accident
1107	Alexander I accedes in Scotland
1124	David I accedes in Scotland
1135	Stephen accedes in England but there is civil war 1139–1148
1136	Welsh defeat Normans at Battle of Crug Mawr
1153	Malcolm IV accedes in Scotland. Treaty of Wallingford secures succession for Henry II
1154	Nicholas Breakspear becomes only English pope (Adrian IV). Henry II accedes in England
1165	William I accedes in Scotland
1167	Oxford University founded
1169	Strongbow arrives in Ireland
1170	Murder of Thomas Beckett
1171	Henry II arrives in Ireland–Lordship of Ireland created
1176	First Eisteddfod held at Aberteifi
1189	Richard I accedes in England.
1199	John accedes in England
1209	Cambridge University founded
1214	Alexander II accedes in Scotland
1214	Battle of Bouvines. John loses Normandy and Brittany
1215	Magna Carta sees limiting of king's pwers by the barons
1216	Henry III accedes in England aged

nine. William Marshal acts as regent

1249 Alexander III accedes in Scotland

1263 Battle of Largs, although inconclusive, sees Alexander III halt the Vikings. Next year he invaded the Hebrides.

1264 Henry III calls first parliament

1264 Battle of Lewes where Simon de Montfort captures king

1265 Battle of Evesham. Defeat of de Montfort by Prince Edward (later Edward I)

1266 At Treaty of Perth Hebrides are sold to Scotland

1267 Henry III acknowledges Llywelyn ap Gruffydd's position as Prince of Wales

1272 Edward I accedes in England

1284 Principality of Wales incorporated into England under the Statute of Rhuddlan

1286 Margaret accedes to the throne of Scotland but dies in 1290 in Orkney. Edward I chosen to arbitrate the Scottish succession

1292 John of Balliol chosen to be king of Scotland

1295 Scotland and France ally

1296 Balliol deposed in Scotland

1296 Edward I defeats Scottish at Battle of Dunbar

1298 Edward I defeats William Wallace at Battle of Falkirk

1301 Edward I's eldest son becomes Prince of Wales. All future eldest sons (other than Edward III) take the title

1305 William Wallace executed

1306 Robert I the Bruce accedes in Scotland

1307 Edward II accedes in England in England

1314 Robert the Bruce defeats Edward II at Bannockburn

1316 Edward Bruce leads expedition to Ireland

1327 Edward II deposed and murdered. Edward III accedes in England. Regency by his mother Isabella and Mortimer

1329 David II accedes in Scotland

1330 Edward III captures and executes Mortimer

1337 Start of the Hundred Years' War

1340 Naval Battle of Sluys where French/Castilian fleet beaten by English

1346 Battle of Crécy sees Edward III defeat Philip VI of France

1349 Black Death reaches Britain. Some 900,000 people die–possibly up to a third of the population

1356 Battle of Poitiers–the Black Prince defeats and captures John II of France

1364 Death of John II in captivity. Charles V succeeds and drives English out of most of France

1371 Robert II accedesin Scotland

1376 Black Prince dies. His son, Richard, becomes heir

1377 Richard II accedes in England on death of his grandfather

1381 Peasants Revolt

1387 Canterbury Tales produced

1390 Robert III accedes

1399 Henry IV accedes in England after Richard "resigns" the throne to him. He dies in prison around 1400

1400 Owain Glyndŵr's revolt begins

1406 James I accedes in England

1412 Defeat of Owain Glyndŵr by Prince Henry

1413 Henry V accedes in England

1414 St. Andrews founded

1415 French defeated at Battle of Agincourt

1420 Treaty of Troyes. Apogee of British power in France

1422 Henry VI accedes in England

1429 Joan of Arc lifts siege of Orleans, leads to Battle of Patay where French rout the English

1430 Joan captured and executed in 1431

1437 James II accedes in Scotland

1450 English defeated by the French at Formigny. English territories, except Calais, fall to France

1451 Glasgow University founded

1453 Battle of Castillon sees final defeat of English to end the Hundred Years' War

1455 Wars of the Roses begin at Battle of St. Albans

1460 James III accedes in Scotland

1461 Edward IV takes the throne after Battle of Towton, the bloodiest battle ever in Britain

1471 Final Lancastrian defeat at Tewkesbury and murder of Henry VI

1483 Edward V is murdered in the Tower, probably by Richard III, leading to latter's accession

1485 Richard defeated at Bosworth Field and victorious Henry Tudor starts a new dynasty

1488 James IV accedes in Scotland

1503 James IV marries Margaret daughter of Henry VII

1509 Henry VIII accedes

1513 James V accedes in Scotland after father killed at Battle of Flodden Field following invasion of England

1521 Henry granted title Defender of the Faith by Pope Leo X

1533 Official marriage of HenryVIII to

Anne Boleyn. Marriage with Catherine declared invalid and Elizabeth declared heir.

1534 Act of Supremacy–monarch declared head of church in Britain. Dissolution of the Monasteries

1541 Henry changes title from Lord of Ireland to King of Ireland

1542 Mary I Queen of Scots accedes at six days old

1547 Edward VI accedes in England. Lady Jane Grey named heir but Mary takes power after nine days. Jane is beheaded in 1554

1554 Mary marries the future Philip II of Spain

1558 Calais is lost to the French. Elizabeth I accedes in England

1580 Francis Drake returns from circumnavigating the world

1587 Mary, Queen of Scots executed

1588 Spanish Armada defeated

1598–1603 Rebellion in Ireland–the Nine Years War.

1603 James I (James VI of Scotland) succeeeds to throne, uniting Britain under one monarch

1605 Gunpowder Plot foiled

1607 Colony at Jamestown, Virginia established

1609 Plantation of Ulster by English and Scttish protestants

1620 Pilgrim Fathers sail for America

1625 Charles I accedes in England

1629 Parliament dissolved: start of Eleven Years' Tyranny

1642 Civil War begins

1648 Cromwell destroys Royalists and Scots at Preston

1649 Beheading of Charles I

1651 Charles II crowned in Scotland but defeated at Worcester and goes into exile

1653 Protectorate declared

1658 Oliver Cromwell dies; succeeded by son Richard

1660 Charles II restored to the throne

1662 Mary Stuart marries William of Orange

1685 James II accedes; defeats Charles II's illegitimate son, the Duke of Monmouth, at Sedgemoor

1688 "Glorious Revolution" sees William of Orange land at Torbay. James II takes flight.

1689 William III & Mary II are declared king and queen. James II lands forces in Ireland

1690 William III defeats James II at the Battle of the Boyne

1692 Massacre of Glencoe

1694 Mary dies leaving William to rule alon. English, Dutch and Austrians ally against Louis XIV

1701 Act of Settlement nominates House of Hanover as heirs

1702 Anne accedes in England

1704 John Churchill, Duke of Marlborough, defeats French at Blenheim

1707 Union of England and Scotland

1714 George I accedes in England

1715 First Jacobite rebellion to put James II's son on throne fails

1727 George II accedes in England

1743 George II becomes the last British monarch to lead his army into battle at Dettingen

1745 Final Jacobite rebellion ends in a bloody massacre at Culloden

1750 The Highland Clearances begin

1756 The Seven Years' War begins

1757 Battle of Plassey secures British control of India

1760 George III accedes in England

1773 Boston Tea Party

1775 American War of Independence begins

1781 Battle of Yorktown. General Cornwallis surrenders and the American colonies are lost. Loyalists flee to Canada

1788 First publication of the *Times* newspaper

1793 Start of war with France

1798 Wolf Tone and the the Society of United Irishmen rebel against British rule in Ireland

1801 United Kingdom created. Irish parliament dissolved

1805 Nelson's victory at Trafalgar defeats Franco-Spanish navy

1815 Battle of Waterloo sees Napoleon finally defeated

1820 George IV accedes in England

1830 William IV accedes in England

1833 Abolition of the slave trade in England

1837 Victoria accedes in England

1845 Irish potato famine leads to huge loss of life and a diaspora

1861 Prince Albert dies

1876 Victoria becomes Empress of India

1901 Edward VII accedes in England. Birth of the Labour Party

1903 Women's Social and Political Union founded to promote universal suffrage for women

1910 George V accedes in England

1914–1918 The Great War. Britain declares war after German advance into Belgium

1916 Easter Rising in Ireland

1918 Spanish flu epidemic

1919 Lady Astor becomes first female MP in England

1921 Anglo-Irish peace treaty leads to partition of Ireland

1922 Irish Civil War

Index

NB: page numbers in *italic* indicate illustrations